Horrible
Facts

Horrible Facts

The truth has never been more disgusting!

Published and distributed by
TOBAR LIMITED
The Old Aerodrome, Worlingham, Beccles,
Suffolk, NR34 7SP, UK

www.tobar.co.uk

This edition printed 2011

Author: Anne Rooney

ISBN 13: 978-1-903230-34-3
CH001264EN
Supplier 03, Date 0811, Print run 1270

Printed in China

contents

intRoDuctiOn

Did you know that in some places people eat rotten food, not because they forgot to go to the shop, but because they actually like it? Or that in other places, people don't let their dead rest in peace, but keep them up at all hours joining in with family celebrations? And do you know what's living inside your body – apart from you?

Would you like to find out? Then this is the book for you! Some facts might make you feel a bit queasy, so try to have a bucket (or a sickbag) handy at all times!

FeeLing Sick Yet?

No, you say? Well, here are some free extra facts all about… well, sick bags! Just to get you in the right mood:

Virgin Atlantic Airways once got top designers to work on its airsickness bags. The cost of a full set of these 20 stylish sick bags has been known to reach triple figures.

You can buy rare airsickness bags on eBay.

The world's largest collection of airsickness bags is owned by Niek Vermeulen of the Netherlands, who has 3,728 of them, from 802 airlines.

A British Airways airsickness bag from 1996 has instructions (for what? Vomiting?) in 11 languages, which is a record, apparently.

There is an e-mail group for people who want to swap (unused) airsickness bags.

Now, ready to cringe? Then read on …

BODY

FacTS

The acid in your stomach is so strong that it can dissolve steel razor blades – it's still not a good idea to eat them, though!

Anne Boleyn, one of King Henry VIII's six wives, had six fingers on each hand and an extra nipple. This was claimed to be evidence of witchcraft and was used in her trial when Henry had her executed in 1536.

in the old days, children being trained as acrobats for circuses were strapped into strange and often very painful positions to make their bodies more bendy.

Egyptian mummies that have been dead for 3,000 years still have their fingerprints intact.

a beef tapeworm, caught from eating eggs in infected beef, can grow to 12 metres (39 feet) long in the human gut.

More than 100 million micro-organisms live in your mouth at any time.

The average person loses 200 millilitres (7 fluid ounces) of water a day in his or her faeces.

You turn white when you're really scared because blood drains from your skin. This protected primitive humans from bleeding to death if bitten by scary, wild animals.

in 1970, a thief was caught in Zurich, Switzerland, when a finger that had been cut off by broken glass at the crime scene was matched to his finger prints in police records.

Girls who made matches in the 1800s often suffered from *phossy jaw* – their jaw bones would rot away, poisoned by the phosphorus used to make the matches.

The mawworm can grow to 30 centimetres (1 foot) and then come out of the body from any gap or hole, including the corner of the eye.

If you could scrunch together all the bacteria living on the outside of your body, they would take up about the same amount of space as one pea.

In 1973, Italian kidnappers were paid a ransom of over $3 million (about £2 million) after they cut off the ear of their kidnap victim and sent it to his very rich grandfather, John Paul Getty.

If your vomit looks like what you've just eaten, that's exactly what it is. If it's soupy, then it's because it's been in your stomach for a while.

Long ago, rich people used to pay for healthy teeth to be pulled from poor people – often teenagers – and implanted in their own jaws when their rotten teeth were removed.

Pinworms cause an itchy bottom because they sneak out at night to lay their eggs there.

All the bacteria living inside your body would fill six teaspoons.

When diarrhoea turns pale, it contains bits of the lining of your gut.

Dentists in the Far East used to pull teeth out with their bare hands! In China, they practiced by pulling nails out of wood with their fingers.

Urine doesn't contain bacteria. Becalmed or shipwrecked sailors used to drink it with no ill effects.

Ten billion scales of skin fall off your body every day.

Your body needs sleep. Staying awake for two weeks can be enough to kill you.

Foods that will make you fart include beans, bran, broccoli, sprouts, cabbage, cauliflower and onions.

Adult feet produce about a quarter of a cup of sweat a day from 250,000 pores – wait four days and you could make a cup of foot-sweat tea!

Horrible Facts

at least 1.3 billion people are infected
with a small hookworm that attaches
to the inside of the gut. A lot of attached
hookworms look like fur or a thick carpet.
Around the world, they suck a total of 10
million litres (around 21 million pints) of
blood a day.

The larvae of the pork tapeworm, hatched
from eggs eaten in infected pork, can travel
around the body and live in the brain, eyes, heart
or muscles.

an Indian man known as **Snake Manu**
can put small snakes, including deadly
cobras, into his mouth and pass them out
through his nose.

In ancient Mexico, people bound their
babies' heads tightly to make their skulls
long and thin.

about a third of your faeces is not old
food, but bacteria that help you to
digest food, and bits of the lining of the
inside of your gut.

When a wound gets infected, it oozes yellow pus. Pus is a mixture of dead blood cells, bacteria and other dead cells from your body.

Prickly heat rash is caused by sweat sticking to the layer of dead skin cells on top of your skin. Since the cells can't fall off, the sweat can't escape and makes the live cells underneath swell up.

Most people have *mites* – very tiny creatures related to spiders – living in their eyelashes, eyebrows, ears, and noses.

For a work entitled *Self*, created in 1991, English sculptor Marc Quinn made a copy of his head, moulded from his own deep-frozen blood. Quinn collected almost 4 litres (8 pints) of his blood over five months, poured it into a mould of his head and froze it.

Surma girls of Ethiopia put clay disks in their lower lip, stretching the lip outwards. The size of the disk indicates how many cattle a man needs to provide to marry the girl – they can be up to 15 centimetres (6 inches) across.

Pilgrims to the Tirupati temple in India give some of their hair as a sacrifice. The temple employs 600 barbers who work day and night to shave pilgrims, taking 6.5 million gifts of hair a year. The hair is then sold to wigmakers and for use as fertilizer.

In some parts of Africa and on some Pacific islands, people make patterns of raised scars on their skin as a decoration or to show their bravery. The wounds are made with sharp spikes or thorns from plants and often rubbed with special kinds of earth or leaves to created coloured tattoos.

The wucheria worm can live in the lymph system and grow up to 12 centimetres (5 inches) long.

About 70 millilitres (around 2.5 fluid ounces) of blood are spurted out of your heart with each beat.

It's possible to get dandruff in your eyebrows as well as in the hair on top of your head.

In some countries, the umbilical cord – the cord that attaches the unborn baby to its mother – is dried and kept after birth, to use in spells or medicines.

Dust mites are found in all houses. They eat the dead skin we shed all the time, and live in beds, carpets, rugs and anywhere else snug that collects flakes of skin.

People who lose an arm or leg in an accident or operation can often still feel it hurting, aching or itching, but can do nothing to make it feel better.

If you unravelled all the tiny tubes in your kidneys and laid them end to end, they would stretch 80 kilometres (50 miles). Yet they scrunch up to fit into kidneys only 10 centimetres (4 inches) long.

Each year, 6,500 people are taken to British hospitals after being injured by a lawnmower. Injuries include the slicing off of a toe or even a finger!

The old Chinese medical technique of acupuncture involves sticking lots of very thin needles into a person's body. The theory is that putting the needles on 'energy pathways' around the body relieves pain and cures illness.

You will produce 45,000 litres (about 95,000 pints) of urine in your life – enough to fill a small swimming pool!

athlete's foot is a fungus that grows in the warm, sweaty spaces between your toes. It causes uncomfortable itching and cracked skin.

Head lice can change colour to blend in with the hair they are hiding in.

Liposuction is a popular operation in Europe and the USA amongst people who feel they are too fat. A surgeon sticks a long, hollow needle into the fat part – such as the tummy or thighs – uses ultrasound to turn the fat to yellow mush, and then sucks it out through the needle.

The medical name for earwax is *cerumen*; the sticky substance is produced by more than 4,000 glands in your ears.

Urine is a good remedy for jellyfish stings, so if you're standing in the sea and get stung, remember to urinate down your legs.

Chewing gum and using straws both make you burp more since they encourage you to swallow air.

The palms of the hands are the sweatiest parts of the body, followed by the feet.

When ancient Egyptians mummified someone, they used a special long-handled spoon to scoop the brains out through the dead person's nose. Instead of letting it go to waste, they often fed the brain to animals.

if you don't brush plaque off your teeth, it hardens into a substance called *tartar* which is like cement and impossible to remove with your toothbrush.

Horrible Facts

The Bedouin people in the Middle East consider it polite to burp after a meal.

Hair grows all over your body except the palms of your hands, the soles of your feet and your lips.

A single drop of blood contains 250 million blood cells.

A facelift to remove wrinkles involves cutting away part of the skin, pulling the remainder tight again and stitching it in place.

Some people have injections of collagen to 'plump up' their wrinkles. The collagen – a fibre found in skin – is usually taken from pigs or cows.

If you never wear shoes, the skin on the soles of your feet eventually thickens and hardens so that you can walk over sharp stones without hurting yourself.

Vomiting a lot can give you a black eye – the pressure can burst the blood vessels around your eyes.

if you could line up all your blood cells – all 25 billion of them – they would go round the world four times.

A bruise is caused by bleeding under your skin. The blood can't get out if there isn't a cut, so it just leaks out – it's purple because that's the colour of blood that doesn't have any oxygen in it.

even bald people have very fine hair on their head, called *vellus*.

The Binderwur tribe in India used to kill and eat sick and old people to please their goddess Kali.

The proper, medical name for burping is *eructation*.

Romans used to clean their teeth with urine, and it was used as a mouthwash until the 1800s in Europe.

21

The gunge that collects in your belly button is a mix of dirt, dead skin cells and oils from your body.

Your belly button is formed from the shrivelled up stump of the umbilical cord – the tube that connected you to your mother's body before you were born.

Over a ton of pubic hair has to be filtered out of London's sewage each year and removed to landfill sites.

A very fat person who flushes an aeroplane toilet while still sitting on it can have his or her rectum sucked out by the pull of the toilet's flush.

Most people fart about 14 times a day. That's a lot of gas!

Human hair grows about just over a centimetre (half an inch) a month.

air you swallow, and gas released from food as you digest it, comes out as a burp or a fart – which one depends on how far through your intestines it has got.

The botfly lays its eggs on a mosquito, and they hatch when the mosquito bites someone. The maggot grows for six weeks in a lump called a *warble* under the persons' skin until it pops out when it's fully grown.

expert botfly squeezers (employed to remove botfly maggots from people) can shoot a botfly from an infected swelling distances of 3 metres (10 feet) or more. Quite a skill!

When you die, the bacteria in your gut start to eat away at you from the inside.

a man with the stage name of Enigma has had surgery to give him horns on his head. He is hoping to get a tail sometime in the future.

The best recorded distance for projectile vomiting is 8 metres (27 feet)!

a scab forms because cells in your blood called platelets make a very thin fibre that traps other blood cells and holds them in a layer that dries out over a scratch or cut.

In some parts of the world, people wear extremely heavy earrings to weigh their ears down and stretch the lobes. The earrings can weigh up to half a kilogram (1 pound) and hang from huge, long holes in the ear lobe.

R hinotillexomania is the scientific word for picking your nose.

When you breathe normally, air goes into your nose at about 6.5 kilometres (4 miles) per hour. When you take a good sniff at something, it goes in at 32 kilometres (20 miles) per hour. When you sneeze, it comes out at 160 kilometres (100 miles) per hour!

if you could lay out all your blood vessels
end to end they would go around the
world more than twice.

You swallow about 1 litre (2 pints) of mucus
(snot) every day.

at any one time, parasites account for
one hundredth of your body weight.

the mental disorder called *walking corpse
disease* leads people to believe that parts
of their body are missing or that they are dead.

Hookworms can infest people who walk
barefoot. They bore through the skin
of the feet and travel in the blood to the
lungs, where they come out and crawl up
to the throat, to be swallowed and start a
new life in the gut.

there is enough iron in the human body to
make a nail.

Your body absorbs about two-thirds of
the volume of the food you eat – the
rest is squished into faeces.

A dead body quickly looks greyish since the blood drains down to the part of the body closest to the ground. The effect is most noticeable in people with white skin.

N ight-handed people sweat most under their right arm; left-handed people sweat most under their left arm.

P eople who live in big cities make more earwax than those who live in the country, where the air is cleaner.

N early half the dust in your house – and what is vacuumed up when you clean the house – is old skin cells!

Y our intestines are about four times your height – they fit because they're all squashed up and coiled around.

N ose pickings are a mix of drying mucus and rubbish filtered out of the air you breathe in – pollen, dust, smoke, dirt, sand, and even tiny particles of dust from space!

The infection *thrush* can cause a white, hairy fungus to grow on the tongue.

Dandruff is a mixture of dirt and dead skin cells stuck together with oil that oozes out of your glands on your head. If your head oozes too much oil, your dandruff becomes noticeable.

Babies can get extra-thick, yellow dandruff that sticks to their heads in scales. It's called *cradle cap* and is more noticeable because they usually don't have much hair.

A person produces 1.5 litres (2.6 pints) of spit (saliva) every day and swallows almost all of it.

The toilet paper that Americans use in one day would go around the world nine times.

The skin of an adult laid out flat on the floor would cover about 1.67 square metres (18 square feet).

Beards grow faster than any other body hair. If a man never cut his beard, it would grow 9.1 metres (30 feet) in his lifetime.

Your heart pumps around 182 million litres (48 million gallons) of blood in your lifetime – with an endless supply of blood, it could fill a swimming pool in less than a month!

You lose 80 hairs from your head every day – but you have about 100,000 so don't worry, you won't start to look bald just yet. And they regrow quickly when you're young.

a very long sneezing fit can cause a heart attack.

When you sneeze, all your body functions stop – even your heart stops beating.

If you could spread out your lungs on the ground, unravelling all the tiny little pockets, they would cover a tennis court.

When you blush, your stomach blushes too! A blush sends blood flooding into the tiny blood vessels on your face and also to the many blood vessels inside your stomach.

One in 100,000 people is born with an extra finger on each hand, but usually they are only small stumps.

When you vomit, the same muscle movements that push food down through your gut to be digested go into reverse, pushing it back up again.

Most people produce about 1.7 litres (3 pints) of urine a day.

A spot or pimple is caused by a waxy oil called *sebum* and tiny bits of dead skin collecting in a little hole in your skin. It goes black if it gets big enough to force your pore open and let air in. When bacteria start to eat away at the gunk, a red spot grows with nasty yellow pus inside.

Sometimes, if a person's eye comes out of its socket in an accident and dangles on their cheek, that person can push it back in with no lasting ill effects.

It can take up to two days for food to pass through your body – from going in your mouth to coming out your bottom.

The longest tapeworm ever found in a human was 33 metres (around 108 feet) long.

Danish astronomer Tyco Brahe wore a metal nose because his own fell off after he suffered from the disease *syphilis*.

Roundworm is the most common gut parasite in the world. It looks rather like an earthworm, and you can catch it by eating food contaminated with faeces.

If you laid out the airways in your lungs in a long line, they would stretch over 2,400 kilometres (1,500 miles).

a smelly fart contains the same gas that makes rotten eggs stink – *hydrogen sulphide.*

If too much wax builds up in your ears, a doctor can soften it and then scoop it out with a special spoon called a *curette.*

If you took all the nerves out of an adult's body and laid them end to end they would stretch 75 kilometres (47 miles). But the adult would not be pleased.

When you sleep, you aren't blinking so there is no way to sweep away the mix of water, oils and other chemicals that wash over your eyes. Instead, they dry out around the edges of your eyes making crispy or slimy yellow gunk.

The sores caused by the disease *typhus* can rot the flesh, sometimes causing toes and fingers to drop off.

Wet hair stretches to about 1.5 times its dry length.

Sweat doesn't actually smell – it's the bacteria breaking it down that produce the pong.

If you have a spitting contest, you'll do better if you can see some food, or even a picture of food. If you can't manage to do that, just thinking about your favourite food will help to make your mouth water.

Men grow ear hair as they get older; women don't.

Food can slosh around in your stomach for up to four hours, churning around like a washing machine.

Feet smell awful sometimes because lots of bacteria and fungi like to live on them – especially if they are hot and wet and sweaty. The bacteria feed on the dead skin and sweat, making smelly gases.

If you throw up and your vomit is greenish, it contains bile from further down in your intestine than just your stomach. The bile and stomach acid make vomit taste awful.

The disease *necrotizing fasciitis* causes the flesh to rot from within and drop off in chunks. Huge holes up to 15 centimetres (6 inches) across can form in sufferers' bodies.

Your eyes make 4.5 litres (8 pints) of tears a year – they keep your eyes wet even if you're not crying.

Slime oozes from the inside of your stomach to keep the acid in the stomach from dissolving its walls and eating into your body – digesting you from the inside.

Stomach gurgling – called *borborygmus* by scientists – is the sound of half-digested food, gas and stomach acid churning around.

after you die, your body starts to dry out and shrink, creating the illusion that your hair and nails are still growing after death.

A gut parasite carried in water infested half a million people in Wisconsin in 1993 when it got into the water supply. A hundred people died.

i f you are close to a really loud noise – a massive volcano erupting, or a huge explosion – the thin, tight skin inside your ear called your eardrum can burst because of the pressure.

T o save space, 98 per cent of dead Japanese people are cremated rather than buried.

i n Palestine, pregnant women who hoped for a son used to drink a potion made from the burned and powdered umbilical cord of a newborn baby boy.

B abies are born without kneecaps – they develop at between two to six years of age.

T here are more germs under your fingernails than on a toilet seat.

When you sneeze, up to a million tiny viruses are sprayed out of your nose and mouth. Just one of these can be enough to infect someone else.

Faeces smell largely because the microbes in your gut produce two stinky chemicals as they work to break down your food – *indole* and *skatole*.

Urine doesn't smell until it hits the air. Then a chemical in it called urea starts to break down into ammonia and the smell begins…

More than 200 types of different organisms live inside or on your body at any time.

Before artificial false teeth were made of porcelain in the 1800s, many people who needed false teeth wore teeth pulled from the mouths of corpses.

People either have pale and dry or dark and sticky earwax. It's an inherited trait, with dry earwax occurring more commonly in Asia, or in people of Asian decent.

William McIloy had 400 operations because he suffered from *Munchausen's syndrome*, which is a mental disorder that makes people want to receive medical treatment. He had to give a false name and move around a lot to get away with it.

King Louis IV of France had a stomach that was twice the size of a normal human stomach.

Chinese leader Mao Tse-Tung never brushed his teeth, giving as a reason that tigers never brushed their teeth either.

a French entertainer in the late 1800s used to make 'music' by farting out tunes. It must have been a stinky show!

The weight of ashes from the average cremated human body is 4 kilograms (9 pounds).

Two thousand glands in your ear make earwax to protect you from getting dirt, dust and germs deep in your ear. The wax slowly hardens and comes to the edge of your ear to fall out. If it doesn't fall out, it can harden into a plug of wax up to 2.5 centimetres (about 1 inch) long.

A man with the stage name Lizardman has slit his tongue in two, from the tip to the middle, so that it is forked. He also has green scales tattooed over his skin.

There is enough fat in the human body to make seven bars of soap.

It takes just over 3 kilograms (7 pounds) of pressure to tear off a human ear – don't try it!

every minute, 30,000 to 40,000 skin cells drop off your body.

Horrible Facts

When you have diarrhoea, instead of absorbing water from your food, your intestines ooze more water into it to rush it through the system and out the other end as a watery mush.

You shed and regrow your skin roughly every 27 days, making a total of about 1,000 complete skins in a lifetime. A person who lives to 70 years of age will shed 47 kilograms (105 pounds) of skin.

A newborn baby produces its own body weight in faeces every 60 hours.

King Louis XIV of France's feet started to rot in his old age. A valet once found a toe that had dropped off in one of the king's socks.

There are more bacteria in your mouth than there are people in the world.

Earwax comes in a range of colours including yellow, grey, brown and pumpkin orange.

An adult human contains enough water to fill three large buckets.

it would take 20 minutes to pour all the human urine produced in a single day over **Niagara Falls.**

If your head is chopped off, you can remain conscious for about 25 seconds!

Queen Isabella of Spain boasted that she only took two baths in her whole life – one when she was born, and one before her wedding.

If your fingers or toes get very cold, they can get frostbite. They slowly rot and turn black, and have to be cut off to keep the rot from spreading any further.

in Scandinavian countries, people used to burn children's first teeth when they fell out in case witches found them and used them to cast an evil spell on the child.

Horrible Facts

The women of the Karen tribe in Thailand traditionally wear masses of metal bands around their necks The first bands are added on a girl's fifth birthday, and more are added every few months. If the bands are removed, the woman's weakened neck muscles can't support her head. Removing the bands became an effective punishment.

An adult has around 5 million hairs on his or her head and body.

While talking, we spit out 300 tiny drops of spit per minute.

Electric signals from the brain can continue for 37 hours after death.

The *scabies mite* burrows inside your skin, making long tunnels, causing terrible itching.

If you try to stop yourself from throwing up by closing your mouth, the vomit will just come out of your nose.

There is enough sulphur in a human body to kill all the fleas on a dog.

You will produce about 33,000 litres (8,700 gallons) of urine in your life.

Godfrey Hill, from the UK, has ten complete fingers and two thumbs and has been accused of being an alien or the Messiah.

The energy from the food you need in one day is just enough to heat four teaspoons of water from freezing to boiling point .

FOOD

an average-sized person eats around 22,700 kilograms (50,000 pounds) of food over the course of his or her life.

Bedouin wedding feasts sometimes include a roast camel, stuffed with a sheep, stuffed with chickens, stuffed with fish, stuffed with eggs.

In the 1800s, it was common to mix ground bones into flour to make it go further. Tasty!

Henry V of England once held a Christmas feast at which the menu included carps' tongues, roasted dolphin and flowers set in jelly.

Honey is bee vomit. Bees drink nectar from flowers which they turn into honey before throwing it back up to store in the hive.

Argentinian gauchos keep a piece of beef under their saddles so that it is pummelled until tender as they ride around all day. It's said that the dish steak tartar came from Mongolian warriors doing the same and then eating the steak raw.

The Roman emperor Nero kept a 'glutton' – an Egyptian slave who ate everything he was given to eat, including human flesh.

To make especially tender beef, the Japanese shut cattle in the dark, feed them beer and employ special cattle masseurs to massage them by hand three times a day.

Stinkheads are a traditional Alaskan dish. Fish heads – often from salmon – are buried in pits lined with moss for a few weeks or months until rotten. They are then kneaded like pastry to mix up all the parts and eaten.

Flavours of ice cream that are available in Japan include octopus, ox tongue, cactus, chicken wing and crab.

In 1919, a tidal wave of molasses swept through Boston, USA. A storage tank burst, spilling 7.5 million litres (2 million gallons) of it into the streets. It poured over houses, knocking them down, in a wave two storeys high.

The Spanish eat cabrales cheese only when it is 'con gusano' – crawling with live maggots.

In India, ants are roasted, ground to a paste and served as chutney.

A stew eaten at a funeral in Stone Age Wales was made from shellfish, eels, mice, frogs, toads, shrews and snakes.

an 18th-century recipe for making an enormous egg suggests sewing 20 egg yolks into an animal bladder, then dropping it into another animal bladder filled with 20 egg whites and boiling it all together.

In Sardinia, cheese is left in the sun for flies to lay their eggs in. When the maggots hatch, the swarming mass is spread on bread and eaten.

Jellyfish are eaten dried and salted in some parts of the world. And in the Gilbert Islands, in the western Pacific Ocean, jellyfish ovaries are served fried.

Condemned prisoners are traditionally allowed a delicious last meal. In some US states, it's not actually their very last meal, but is served a day or two before the execution and is called a 'special meal'.

Odd crisp flavours available around the world include octopus, seaweed, banana and sour cream, and squid.

During the Second World War, people in the UK were urged by the government to make the most of wild foods and were given recipes for cooking roast squirrel, rook casserole, stewed starlings, and baked sparrows.

The Insect Club, a restaurant in the US, serves only dishes made with insects. The menu includes cricket pizza, insect chocolates and 'insects in a blanket' – crickets, mealworms and blue cheese in puff pastry.

In Slovenia, people still raise and fatten dormice, ready to stew.

In Nepal, Tibet, and parts of China, black tea is served with yak butter – butter made from yak milk.

Tradition tells that the French cheese Roquefort was discovered when a shepherd abandoned his lunch in a cave to chase a pretty girl he saw outside. When he returned months later, the old cheese had gone mouldy but still tasted good.

Durian is a fruit the size of a football that is covered in spikes and smells like rotting meat. It's supposed to taste good, though!

Roman banquets often featured hummingbirds cooked in walnut shells and roasted stuffed dormice, sometimes rolled in honey and poppy seeds. The Romans even had farms producing dormice because they were so popular.

During the First World War, Germany suffered such food shortages that people ate dogs and horses and even the kangaroos from the zoos!

In Madagascar, people make a stew from tomatoes and zebras.

Raake orret is eaten in Norway. Trout caught in a freshwater stream are stored in salted water with a little sugar and kept in a cool place, such as the garage, for months before eating.

Ambuyat, eaten in Brunei, is made from pulp from the sago palm, stewed in water for several hours. The same mixture is made to stick the roof on a house!

Also in Brunei, the *sago worm*, which lives inside rotting sago palms, is often cooked and eaten.

In northern Australia, children often eat green ants. Pick them up, squish the head so they don't nibble you, and bite off the body.

P'tcha is an east European Jewish food made by stewing calves' feet until they turn to jelly.

Cinemas in Colombia serve paper cones filled with giant fried or toasted ants.

Pruno is a 'wine' made by **American prisoners** from a mixture of fruit, sugar cubes, water and tomato ketchup, left to fester together in a bin bag for a week. In some prisons, pruno causes so many discipline problems that all fruit has been banned.

In the Japanese countryside, salamanders and skinks are grilled on sticks and served with lettuce for a tasty snack.

a restaurant in Osaka, Japan, serves whale ice cream made from the blubber of the minke whale.

A rat restaurant in China sells rat and snake soup, rat kebabs, steamed rat with rice and crispy fried rat.

in Nicaragua, turtle eggs are eaten raw – slit the leathery skin, add some hot sauce, and suck out the gunk.

In Texas, there's an annual rattlesnake round-up. What to do with all the rattlesnakes? Skin them, gut them, cut them into chunks, cover in batter and deep fry.

In Newfoundland, Canada, seal flipper pie is a traditional dish that marks the end of a seal hunt.

Think cabbage is horrid? In Korea, it is sometimes buried in clay pots with salt for many months before it's eaten – this dish is called *kimchi* and is served with most meals.

alligator kebabs are popular in southern Louisiana, USA.

In Fiji, people starve a pig for a week, then feed it veal when it is very hungry. A few hours later, they kill the pig and remove the half-digested veal, which they cook and eat.

a restaurant in Changsha, China, offers food cooked in human breast milk.

As early as the 9th century, the Basques of Spain hunted whales, and whale tongue was considered a great delicacy.

Oellebroed is a Danish soup made from stale rye bread soaked in water, then boiled with beer and sugar and served with cream. It's possible to buy instant oellebroed powder – just add water.

Another way of cooking snakes in Texas – cut the head off, skin and gut it, poke a stick into the neck, wrap the snake loosely around the stick, and roast over a campfire.

Iguanas are a popular and free food in Central America – they can often be caught in backyards.

Slimy green stuff that looks like mucus is supposedly the best part of a lobster or crayfish. It's found in the head. Some Americans eat the main part of the lobster meat and then suck the head to get the gunge out.

in China, people eat jellied ducks' blood.

Cibreo is an Italian dish that consists of the cooked combs from roosters.

Spam is a luncheon meat used as a filling for sandwiches. At a Spam-cooking contest, one contestant made Spam-chip cookies!

The street markets of Indonesia sell whole, smoked bats.

McDonald's in Hong Kong sells a sweetcorn pie in a sweet pie crust, the same as the apple pies in the West.

An international contest to find the best recipe for cooking earthworms included entries of stews, salads, and soups but was won by a recipe for apple sauce surprise cake. Guess what the surprise was…

Jack Fuller was buried in a pyramid in Sussex, England, in 1811. Local people say that inside it, he is seated at a table with a roast chicken and a bottle of port.

Baby mouse wine, from China, is a bottle of wine packed with baby mice to add flavour.

in Canada, deep-fried cod tongues are a popular dish.

In Ness, Scotland, people kill young gannets – a type of seabird – to eat. The claws are the most highly prized part.

Some Arctic explorers have been poisoned by eating polar bear liver. The polar bear eats so much fish that fatal levels of vitamin D collect in its liver.

A restaurant in Pennsylvania, USA, offers a hamburger that weighs 4 kilograms (9 pounds). No one has yet managed to finish one.

Drunken shrimps, served in China, are live shrimps swimming in a bowl of rice wine. The idea is to catch them with chopsticks and bite the heads off.

Bedouin people cook a camel's hump by burying it underground and lighting a fire over the top of it. When they dig it up and eat it, the top is cooked, but the bottom is still mostly raw and bloody.

The Chinese make a soup from the swim bladder of fish. It's the organ that helps fish to stay at the right depth and upright in the water and is rather spongy.

Fried chicken cartilage is served as a bar snack in Japan.

Marmite, a favourite English spread for toast, is made with the leftover yeasty sludge from brewing beer.

Snake wine in China is a very potent alcoholic drink, spiced with juice from the gall bladder of a live snake.

Crispy fried duck or chicken feet are a delicacy in China. In the USA, whole chicken feet are sometimes pickled or made into soup.

In both Sicily and Japan, people eat the raw *roe* (eggs) of sea urchins.

In the Philippines, the eyes are considered the tastiest part of a steamed fish. Suck out the gloop and spit out the hard cornea.

Eskimos have been known to make seagull wine – put a seagull in a bottle of water, wait for it to go off – drink!

In Hungary, scrambled eggs are fried up with the blood from a freshly slaughtered pig.

Central American wedding feasts often included honeyed ants.

in the southern USA, squirrel brains are cooked still in the head. You then crack the skull and scoop the brains out with fingers and fork.

Nutria are a large rodent that live some of the time in the water. They are a pest in Louisiana, where local authorities are encouraging people to eat them – with little success, since they don't taste too good.

Some prisoners have big appetites. Richard Beavers, executed in Texas in 1994, ate for his last meal: six pieces of French toast with butter and syrup, six barbecued spare ribs, six pieces of bacon (burnt), four scrambled eggs, five sausage patties, French fries with ketchup, three slices of cheese, two pieces of yellow cake with chocolate fudge icing and four cartons of milk.

A traditional London dish is eels boiled and served cold in jelly.

in Wales, rook pie was considered a tasty way to get rid of a bird that might otherwise eat the crops.

Biltong is favoured as a snack by rugby supporters in South Africa. It's dried strips of any meat – elephant, eland, antelope…

in Japan, the blowfish is a delicacy, even though it contains a poison gland that, if not properly removed, kills anyone who eats it.

In Sweden, people make dumplings from flour, reindeer blood and salt.

An omelette costing $1000 (£670) called the Zillion Dollar Lobster Frittata was sold by a restaurant in New York. It contains a whole lobster and 280 grams (10 ounces) of caviar, plus eggs, cream, potatoes and whiskey.

In Indonesia, deep-fried monkey toes are eaten by sucking the meat straight off the bone.

In Georgia, there is a price limit of
$40 (£27) on the last meal a prisoner
can order.

Aztecs gave people who were to be human
sacrifices many last meals – they fattened
them up for up to a year.

In the Philippines, chicken heads may be
made into stew or barbecued whole.

Small songbirds cooked and eaten whole have
been so popular in Italy that many types have
been wiped out completely.

In Sweden and Norway, roast reindeer is
a national dish.

Many cheap meat products such as sausages
and burgers are made from 'mechanically
recovered meat', which consists of a meat slurry
collected from washing bones and mincing up
parts of the dead animal that aren't used for
anything else.

In 1971, a man found the head of a mouse in a bar of chocolate.

The Russian Jewish dish kishke is made by stuffing a chicken skin with flour, butter, and spices and boiling it in chicken stock. Dry it out, then cut it into slices as a snack.

In China and Japan, sheets of dried jellyfish are sold for soaking and turning back into slimy jellyfish ready for cooking.

Ancient Greeks, Egyptians, and Romans all gave condemned prisoners a last meal.

The Chinese eat monster barnacles the size of an adult's fist.

The town of Buñol, in Spain, has an annual tomato fight when up to 25,000 people throw around 100 tonnes (220,000 pounds) of tomatoes at each other. The streets can be flooded up to 30 centimetres (12 inches) deep with juice.

The reproductive organs of sea urchins are eaten raw in many parts of the world, including Japan, Chile and France.

Raw, pickled jellyfish are eaten in the Samoan Islands, in the western Pacific Ocean.

Yeast are tiny fungi (mould), present in bread, beer, and wine. The yeast eat sugar in the ingredients, making the gas that forms the bubbles in beer and wine and the holes in bread.

In the Samoan Islands, the intestines of *sea cucumbers* are sold in jars, steeped in seawater. The sea cucumber is a slithery, tube-like animal and not a cucumber at all. When it's cooked, it is called a *sea slug*.

in the UK, game – wild animals and birds shot in the fields – is often hung until it is 'high', which means it is hung up on a hook until it is starting to go off.

In the Masai Mara in Africa, people drink blood drained from the neck of a live animal with a straw, mixed up with milk.

The alcoholic drink mescal has a cactus maggot preserved in the bottle.

In France, calves' eyes are soaked in water, then boiled and stuffed and finally deep-fried in breadcrumbs.

Most US states don't allow alcohol or tobacco in a prisoner's last meal.

Eels are sold live in markets around the world and killed just before cooking – or before putting in the bag to go home if you don't want the bag wriggling all the way.

The British *black pudding* is a sausage made of congealed pigs' blood with lumps of fat embedded in it. It is often fried and eaten for breakfast.

Baby eels, called elvers, are eaten in parts of Europe, including east England. They are very thin, so lots of them are cooked, all tangled together like spaghetti.

Soft ice cream of the type sold in ice cream vans is given its slithery smoothness by an extract of seaweed.

Orangutan lips used to be a delicacy in Vietnam. Hungry?

in Mexico, the alcoholic drink tequila is often served with a worm in the glass – the worm should be swallowed whole with the drink.

Romany people in Europe and poor peasants used to cook wild hedgehogs by rolling them in mud and baking them in the embers of a fire. When the mud dries, the spines can be peeled off with the mud.

Cow's tongue is often sold with the salivary glands – the parts that make spit – ready for boiling. The tongue can weigh up to 2.3 kilograms (5 pounds).

Horrible Facts

In Europe, some people make blood pudding from the blood of a pig or cow mixed with rice, milk and sugar and then baked.

To make the expensive pâté de foie gras, geese are forcibly fattened with grain so that their liver swells to many times its natural size.

In England, *lampreys* – fierce fish that look like eels – are traditionally cooked in a sauce flavoured with their own blood.

In Central and South America, iguana meat is highly prized.

The French *cervela sausage* is made with the brains of pigs.

Roast dog is sold on the streets of Vietnam. The back half of the dog comes with the tail intact.

Spider wine, from Cambodia, is actually rice wine – the spiders are added later.

Mealworms – golden-coloured larvae that eat grain – are farmed in the USA and sold live in pots of bran for cooking. The bran is for the mealworms to eat while they are waiting, since otherwise they will eat each other.

Caviar is the eggs of the sturgeon fish. It is so valuable that an operation is sometimes used to remove the eggs without harming the fish, which then goes on to make more eggs. Previously, the fish was gutted while still alive so that the eggs could be as fresh as possible.

Sheep's eyeballs are eaten in some Arab countries of North Africa.

Birds nest soup is a delicacy in China. It's made from the nests of a special variety of swift that builds its nest from dried strands of its own spit. The nest is soaked in water to soften it, then any sticks and feathers are removed before it is made into a gluey, sticky soup.

The oldest surviving piece of chewing gum is 9,000 years old.

In China, bear paws are roasted in clay – the fur comes off with the dried clay when they are done.

In France, rats found in wine cellars didn't go to waste, but were sometimes cooked in a sauce flavoured with red wine over a fire of burning wine barrels.

In the 1800s, naturalist Frank Buckland served meals such as mice on toast, roasted parrots and stewed sea slug. He tried to make soup from an elephant's trunk, but even after several days' cooking, it was still too chewy.

The Aztec dish tlacatalalli was a stew made from corn and human beings.

In Texas, armadillos are sometimes roasted in their shells, stuffed with carrots, apples, and potatoes. A crunchy treat!

Once, at a Roman banquet, a slave stabbed the stomach of a roast boar to release a flock of live thrushes.

Truffles are a kind of fungus that grow underground in forests in Europe. Truffle hunters use pigs to smell them out. The best truffles are extremely valuable.

The Akoa pygmy tribe eat elephant meat with a serving of live maggots.

Some Amazonian tribes used to make a special soup using the ground bones of their dead relatives.

in the Middle Ages, a peacock was often roasted with its feathers on. The skin was inflated first to keep the feathers from burning and then pierced when the bird was cooked so that it appeared to be alive when served.

In 1135, King Henry I of England died from eating too many lampreys – a kind of eel that sucks its victims to death.

US Air Force pilot, Captain Scott O'Grady, was shot down over Bosnia in 1995 and survived for six days eating only ants.

Some Jewish people eat the braised udder of a cow. Don't knock it 'till you've tried it!

in some countries where people don't have food processors or forks, mothers first chew up food before putting it into their babies' mouths.

Worms steamed whole in a jelly are a tasty treat in China.

in Vietnam, cobra hearts are a common snack. They can be eaten raw, even still beating, with a small glass of cobra blood or dropped into a glass of rice wine. The kidney is often included as an extra titbit.

Eel skin is so hard to remove that some people pull it off with pliers.

The original recipe for baked beans included bear fat and maple syrup.

Australian aborigines like to eat witchetty grubs – the larvae of the ghost moth – raw and wriggling. Or they can be barbecued on a skewer for a couple of minutes, like a kebab.

Camels' feet are cooked in a light stock and served with vinaigrette. Only the feet of young camels are considered tasty. Camel feet can also be cooked in camel milk.

For his last meal, murderer Victor Feguer chose a single olive.

The Scottish dish haggis is made by cutting up the heart, lungs, liver and small intestine of a calf or sheep and cooking it with suet, oatmeal, onions, and herbs in the animal's stomach.

A restaurant in England recently offered snail porridge on its menu.

In China, sharks' fin soup is made from the salted, sun-dried fins of sharks. It is like a bowl of glue, since the fin contains a lot of gelatine.

In the Faroe Islands, north of the UK, a favourite dish is puffin stuffed with rhubarb.

Roman feasts sometimes included the popular delicacy flamingo tongues.

In China, eggs are buried underground until they go exceptionally bad and are then sold and eaten as '100-year-old' eggs. In fact, they are about two years old. The yolks turn green and the whites turn grey or black.

The Air Force Survival Manual issued to US airmen explains which bugs to eat in an emergency for maximum taste and nutrition.

The last meal of Oklahoma City bomber Timothy McVeigh was almost a litre (2 pints) of mint chocolate-chip ice cream.

Honey found in ancient Egyptian tombs has been tasted by archaeologists and found to still be edible, even after thousands of years.

If you eat too many carrots, it's possible that you will turn orange.

Fried crickets are a favourite food in China. Yummy!

The Japanese make natto by leaving soybeans to rot in straw until slimy and sticky – and very smelly.

Some Amazonian people eat omelettes made from tarantula eggs.

Iowa State University's Department of Entomology has published recipes for cooking with insects, including banana worm bread, crackers and cheese dip with candied crickets, and mealworm fried rice.

Australian supermarkets sell tins of witchetty grub soup.

In France, over 40,000 metric tons (88 million pounds) of snails are consumed every year.

Mealworms are supposed to taste better if cooked while still alive.

Blood soup is popular in many parts of the world. In Poland, people eat a duck blood soup called czarnina; in Korea, pig blood curd soup is called seonjiguk; and in the Philippines people eat a pig blood stew called dinuguan.

Sea slug is eaten in China and Spain. It's often sold dried and has to be soaked to restore it to its slimy, squishy glory.

Water cockroaches are roasted and eaten in China – leave the wings and legs.

In Mexico, a black fungus that infects maize is canned and sold. It looks like black slime with a few yellow lumps in.

When a pig is roasted in Cuba, the skull is cracked open and each guest takes a spoon to share scoops of brain.

Sun-dried maggots have been eaten from China to North America.

In Ghana, half of the locally produced meat comes from rats.

In China, people get their own back on poisonous scorpions by frying them and eating the. They are said to taste rather like cashew nuts.

Oysters are always eaten raw – alive – in the UK and US.

In Cambodia, giant grilled spiders are a popular street snack.

The Korean delicacy *sannakji* consists of still-wriggling slices of octopus tentacle.

In the Philippines, fertilized duck or chicken eggs are cooked and eaten – with the unhatched chick partly grown inside. It's called *balut*, in case you want to avoid it on the menu.

Delicacies enjoyed in Iceland include puffin and *svie* – singed and boiled sheep's head.

Native Alaskan Indians bury salmon eggs in a jar for 90 days and eat them when they are truly rotten.

Until 1999, it was legal to enjoy *ortolan* in France – a tiny, rare, songbird, fattened in a dark box to three times it normal size then drowned in brandy and spit roasted for a few minutes before being eaten whole, innards included. (It was OK to leave the head and beak.) Traditionally, it was eaten with a napkin draped over your head and the plate so that none of the delicious smell could escape.

In Palau, an island in the western Pacific Ocean, whole fruit bats, complete with skin, may be ordered as a starter or main course.

In Finland, people cook blood pancakes.

at the winter festival of Thorrablot, Icelanders eat *hákarl* – rotten shark. Shark meat is buried in the ground for six to eight weeks then dried in the open air for two months.

Kakambian, a dish from the Philippines, is made of diced goat – skin, hair, fat and meat all mixed together.

In some parts of Asia, monkey brains are a delicacy – but it's a myth that they are eaten from the head while the monkey is still alive.

In Mongolia, camel or horse milk is stored in a cleaned horse stomach or hide bag and hung up in the *ger* (tent). Everyone who passes the door has to stir or hit the bag. It slowly ferments into a slightly alcoholic, cheesy yoghurt drink that everyone drinks, even children.

In Korea, it's possible to buy canned silkworm pupae, or bags of silkworms from street vendors. The idea is to crunch the end off the grub and suck out the delicious juices...

Bagoong is a very smelly, fermented paste made from mashed shrimps and eaten in the Philippines.

Rocky Mountain oysters, or 'prairie oysters', are calves' testicles – enjoyed fried in parts of the USA.

Morcilla is a Puerto Rican sausage made with rice boiled in pigs' blood, stuffed into a sausage skin and then fried.

In Ecuador, a family barbecue can include guinea pig and snake kebabs.

People in ancient China ate mice as a delicacy.

In Brazil, people eat barbecued armadillo.

In southern Africa, large caterpillars called *mopani* can be bought in tins.

In Hubei Province, China, eels are served whole. The correct way to eat one is to bite through just behind the head and pull out the insides with chopsticks.

In Hong Kong, you can buy packets of crispy fried crabs like packets of crisps.

The Japanese dish shiokara is made by fermenting squid in old fish guts.

In some rural parts of China, you can tuck in to a bowl of owl soup.

in 1973, a Swedish sweets salesman was buried in a coffin made of chocolate.

In North Africa, people eat fried termites.

an American delicacy called headcheese, similar to British brawn, is made by cooking a whole cow or pig head into a mush and letting it cool into a jelly-like mass.

The pearl fish swims into a sea cucumber's anus and lives inside it during the day, coming out at night. The sea cucumber breathes through its anus, so it can't keep the fish out!

The glass frog has a transparent body – its blood vessels, stomach, and beating heart are all visible.

a scorpion can go for a whole year without eating.

As cockroaches grow, they develop a new skin inside their old one, eventually splitting the old one. This new skin is white until it hardens in the air and becomes dark.

Spiders inject flies and bugs with a chemical that paralyzes them and dissolves their insides. The spider then sucks out the liquid since it can't chew.

There are more than 70,000 types of slug and snail in the world. Let's hope they never hold a big party!

The viperfish has teeth so long, it can't close its mouth and it has to open its jaws out flat before it can swallow. Its teeth are half the length of its head!

The skin of a hippopotamus measures about 4 centimetres (1.5 inches) thick. That's about 3.5 centimetres (over an inch) thicker than human skin.

The *banded tenrec*, a kind of hedgehog from Madagascar, sometimes eats so many worms, bugs, and slugs that it makes itself sick.

Sharks will eat almost anything. The stomachs of dead sharks have been found to contain pieces of boats and vehicles and even a complete knight in armour.

Bone-eating zombie worms live on the decaying bodies of dead whales. They have no gut but bore deeply into the bones. Microbes inside the worms digest chemicals sucked out of the bones.

A mosquito can drink one-and-a-half times its own weight in blood at a single meal. Yuck!

a shark can taste blood over a kilometre (about half a mile) away.

In the time of the dinosaurs, there were giant scorpions nearly a metre (3 feet) long. That's bigger than the average domestic dog!

a spider that isn't hungry will wrap up extra bugs in its web to keep for later.

There are 3,500 known species of cockroach. Are others out there? We don't know yet...

if a rat didn't keep chewing, its lower teeth would eventually grow through its top jaw and up into the roof of its mouth.

Every year, 4.5 million litres (1 million gallons) of dog urine goes into the parks of London, England. Stinky!

Carrying garlic might repel mosquitoes rather than vampires.

A planarian worm will regrow its other half if cut in two. If two planarians are cut in half, they can get mixed up and re-attach to the wrong half.

Salamander larvae change form, becoming killer predators, if they sense the vibrations created in water by swimming tadpoles. They grow longer, stronger bodies and broader heads so that they can kill and eat the tadpoles.

Owls' eyes are too large to move in their eye sockets, so they've developed the ability to turn their heads around further than other birds are able to.

Flesh flies eat nothing but old meat and rotting flesh on dead bodies.

Some geckos have no eyelids – they lick their eyeballs to clean them!

Horrible Facts

Scorpions glow in the dark under ultraviolet light.

The vampire squid has the largest eyes of any animal for its body size. The squid is 28 centimetres (11 inches) long and its enormous eyes are 2.5 centimetres (1 inch) across. The equivalent would be a person with eyes the size of table tennis bats!

The job of guard termites is to defend the termite nest or mound. Sometimes they explode in their efforts to deter attackers.

A lion's mane jellyfish is about 2.5 metres (8 feet) across with tentacles 60 metres (200 feet) long. Their poisonous sting can cause an agonizing death.

a duck-billed platypus can stuff its cheek pouches with 600 worms.

An octopus has to turn itself inside out to eat, since its mouth is hidden in between its tentacles.

The leopard seal sometimes attacks people, lunging up through the ice to snap at their feet.

The carpet viper kills more people in the world than any other type of snake. Its bite leads to uncontrollable bleeding.

Cockroaches taste through their feet.

A baby naked mole rat has transparent skin – you can see its insides right through its skin!

The southern giant petrel, a bird that lives near the South Pole, spits globs of oil and regurgitated food at its enemies.

Copepods are tiny crustaceans that swim around in groups of up to a trillion. They are the only known creature that has just one eye.

The wood frog that lives in the Arctic Circle can stay deep-frozen for weeks and survive.

Horses often chew at fly eggs and maggots on their legs and end up swallowing them, so they get a stomach full of crawling maggots.

Nose bots are maggots that live inside the noses of animals that graze, such as sheep, cows, and horses.

The Gila monster is a lizard from South America and Mexico. Although it's only about half a metre (2 feet) long, its bite is so strong that the only way to detach one that's bitten you is to drown it.

Sharks don't have a urinary tract, so their urine leaks out of their skin.

A rat can fall from a five-storey building and walk away unharmed.

Rats have super-strong teeth. Among other things, they can bite through wood, metal and electric cables.

The only mammals that don't get lice are anteaters, armadillos, bats, duck-billed platypuses, whales, dolphins, and porpoises.

The deep-sea gulper eel can eat fish larger than itself. It can open its mouth so wide that its jaw bends back on itself at an angle of more than 180 degrees.

The caterpillar of the polyphemus moth in North America eats 86,000 times its own birthweight in the first 56 days of its life. It's equal to a human baby eating 270 metric tonnes (nearly 600,000 pounds) of food!

a cockroach can survive being frozen in a block of ice for two days.

A pregnant scorpion will sometimes reabsorb its babies instead of giving birth to them.

Mosquitoes in the Arctic hatch when the snows thaw, sometimes making such large swarms they blot out the sun.

Chameleons can change their skin colour to hide themselves (camouflage) – but they also change colour according to mood. Some turn grey when depressed.

instead of eyelids, some geckos have a transparent coating over their eyes. It stays permanently closed but allows the gecko to see anyway.

The bulldog ant from Australia will sting again and again while holding on with its fierce jaws. It can kill a human in 15 minutes.

Head lice suck blood for about 45 seconds every 2–3 hours, but they can go without a meal for up to two days if they are between heads – on a comb, towel, or pillow.

A kind of yellow-bellied toad can produce a nasty foam that smells just like garlic to deter attackers.

Komodo dragons are lizards 3 metres (10 feet) long. They aren't poisonous, but there are so many bacteria in their mouths – growing in rotten meat between their teeth – that a bite from one often leads to blood poisoning and death.

The naked mole rat is perhaps the ugliest mammal in the world. It looks like a wrinkly sausage with very short legs and huge, protruding teeth. It has no hair anywhere except the inside of its mouth.

The bluebottle and greenbottle flies that are common in houses lay their eggs in rotting meat, dead animals and animal faeces.

Bracken Cave in Texas is home to 20 million bats. The floor is caked in a thick layer of bat faeces.

Only female mosquitoes bite and suck blood – they need the protein in blood so that they can lay eggs. The males eat only nectar from flowers.

A maggot doesn't have teeth – it oozes a kind of spit called ferment onto its food. This dissolves the food, and the maggot then sucks it up and tucks in.

a hissing cockroach makes a noise by squeezing air out of tiny holes in its body segments. The sound can be heard 3.7 metres (12 feet) away.

T he *axolotl* is a pale amphibian that is partway between a tadpole and a lizard and lives in a single lake in Mexico. Some axolotls change shape and become land creatures permanently, but most don't ever change.

C rows are one of the few larger creatures that will eat rotting and putrid flesh.

B aby Komodo dragons will eat their brothers and sisters if they are hungry and there is no other food.

i f an octopus loses a tentacle, it can grow a new one.

A stingray has a special cap on the end of its tail that breaks off when it stings, allowing poison to pour out into the wound it's made in its victim.

The *aye-aye* is a nocturnal mammal from Madagascar that has one very long, bony finger on one hand. It looks so frightening that local people believed contact with an aye-aye led to death, so they killed most of them.

Bat faeces lies so deep on the floors of bat caves that people harvest the faeces to sell as fertilizer for plants.

an octopus tentacle will keep wriggling for some time after being cut off.

Mosquitoes have been around for 200 million years. That's so long that even dinosaurs could have been bitten by them!

Flies beat their wings about 180 times a second.

The anglerfish has a glowing blob attached to a spike at the front of its head. In the dark, deep sea, the glowing blob attracts small prey which the anglerfish sucks in and gobbles up.

electric eels can deliver a shock of an incredible 500 volts to stun their dinner into submission.

Flies eat by vomiting up something they've eaten previously so that the chemicals in their vomit can start to dissolve the new meal. When it's sloppy, they suck it all up again. That's why it's a really bad idea to eat anything a fly's been sitting on!

The *guanay cormorant* makes its nest from dried faeces.

Sharks have special organs in their snouts and elsewhere that let them detect the electric fields produced by living animals. They can then home in on the animals to eat them.

a group of jellyfish is called a 'smack'.

A giraffe has special valves in its arteries so that its blood can travel up its neck and reach its head. Without them, it would need a heart as big as its whole body!

a cockroach can withstand more than
120 times the force of Earth's gravity
– an astronaut passes out at 12 times the
pressure of gravity.

L and leeches in Asia can drop from trees onto
people and suck out so much blood, the
person dies.

T he face fly feeds on the mucus
produced in a cow's eyes and nostrils.

S lugs are attracted to beer: some gardeners
trap them by putting out bowls of beer,
which the slugs fall into. They get drunk and
drown. The slugs, not the gardeners!

a 32-kilogram (70-pound) octopus can
squeeze through a hole the size of a
tennis ball.

T he end of a chameleon's tongue can have a
club-like lump oiled with sticky goo, which
helps it to catch insects.

Horrible Facts

The Australian blue-ringed octopus can pump out a poison that will paralyze or kill a human.

When there's not much food around, cockroaches will eat each other – ripping open the victim's stomach and tearing out the insides. Nasty!

Some toads can swallow shrews and mice whole.

Goliath birdeating spiders can grow to the size of a dinner plate and kill small birds.

a head louse can lay 200 to 300 eggs during its life of about 30 days. The eggs only take five to ten days to hatch and start feeding.

Over 100 million years ago, crocodiles were twice the size they are now – up to 12 metres (40 feet) long – and could eat dinosaurs.

Geckos and centipedes both like to eat cockroaches for a tasty meal.

The deadly box jellyfish that lives off the coast of Australia is the size of a basketball but has tentacles that trail 4.5 metres (15 feet). If the tentacles touch you, tiny harpoons inject poison.

a full-grown python can swallow a pig whole.

Baby cockroaches feed on their parents' faeces to get the bacteria they need to help them digest vegetables and other plants.

if a lizard loses its tail, amazingly, it can grow a new one!

A patch of rainforest soil about the size of this book can hatch 10,000 mosquito eggs.

Rabbits partially digest the grass they eat and then excrete it as soft, gluey pellets. They then eat these to finish digesting their meal properly.

Crocodiles carry their young around in their mouths.

The geographic tree frog can change its eyes from brown to patterned to help it camouflage itself in trees.

When a viperfish wants to eat a large meal, it moves all its internal organs towards its tail to make more room inside it for food.

an elephant produces 23 kilograms (50 pounds) of faeces every day.

Vampire bats drink half their body weight in blood every day.

Cat urine glows in the dark (but it has to be very dark, if you're thinking of testing it).

When a fish called the Pacific grenadier is pulled out of the sea by fishermen, the change in pressure makes gas inside it expand quickly and its stomach pops out of its mouth.

a ribbon worm can eat 95 per cent of its own body and still survive.

Light-coloured spots on the surfaces of food show that a fly has vomited something up and tasted the surface; dark-coloured spots are fly faeces.

a cockroach can live for a week after its head is cut off.

Dogs in New York, USA, produce 18 million kilograms (40 million pounds) of faeces a year. Luckily, New Yorkers have to clean up after their dogs.

a leech will suck blood until it is ten times its original size and can't hold any more. Once the leech is full, it drops off its victim.

The *gavial*, a kind of crocodile from India, has over 100 teeth.

Leeches don't only suck from the outside of your body. If you drink water with a leech in, it can attach to the inside of your mouth or throat, and, in a river, leeches can go into your bottom and suck you from the inside.

The potato beetle larva protects itself from birds that want to eat it by covering itself in its own poisonous faeces.

a vampire finch in the Galapagos Islands pecks holes in other birds to feed on their blood.

The turkey vulture excretes faeces onto its legs to keep them cool.

a chameleon's tongue can be twice as long as its body and must be kept curled to fit inside it.

A baby robin eats 4 metres (14 feet) of earthworms a day!

The female black widow spider eats the male after mating, sometimes eating up to 25 partners a day. Now that's a man-eater!

When a toad is sick, it vomits up its own stomach, which hangs out of its mouth for a short time before it swallows it back down.

Some leeches have three mouths, with up to 100 teeth.

Many leeches produce a painkiller so that you don't notice you have been bitten unless you actually see the leech.

The queen naked mole rat is the only one to have babies. She keeps the others sterile (incapable of having babies) using a special chemical in her urine.

A female German cockroach can produce 500,000 young in a year.

Crocodiles can't bite and chew. Instead, they hold their prey underwater to drown it, then twist their bodies around to tear chunks off the victim.

Body lice love dirty places – they were very common in the old days when people didn't wash much, and they often infested soldiers who had to live in dirty conditions. They are most likely to live on your stomach or your anus.

a very stressed octopus will sometimes eat itself.

In some types of anglerfish, the male is much smaller than the female and attaches himself to her body for life. After a while, he becomes fused to her and their body systems combine. His only role is to fertilize her eggs, and he is nourished by her blood.

Vultures gorging themselves on a carcass sometimes eat so much, they can't fly. They then vomit to make themselves lighter.

A dustbin can produce 30,000 flies a week from eggs laid in the rotting rubbish inside.

Vampire bats urinate the whole time they're sucking blood. This ensures they don't get so full of blood they're too heavy to fly. That makes them smarter than vultures, then!

Bird parents eat food for their babies, fly back to the nest, and vomit up the meal into the babies' open beaks.

a single bat can eat 3,000 to 7,000 mosquitoes in a single night; a colony of 500 bats goes through a quarter of a million bugs an hour.

When the *necrophorus beetle* finds a small dead animal, it pushes it into a suitable place, takes some of its fur to make a nest, and lays its eggs near the body.

You could get bitten by a crocodile, but alligators don't like the taste of people.

When the eggs hatch into maggots, they feed on the dead body.

The *slime eel*, or *hagfish*, feeds on dead and dying fish at the bottom of the sea. It enters its victim through the mouth or eye socket and eats it away from the inside, leaving only a bag of skin and bones.

The female praying mantis begins to eat the male during mating; he keeps going, but she eventually eats all of him.

Scorpions paralyze their prey before they suck the juices out. It's not dead, but it can't escape.

Vampire bats don't suck – they make a cut in their victim, then lick the blood as it flows out. To keep it flowing, they have an anticoagulant in their spit – a chemical that keeps blood from clotting and forming a scab.

Some types of octopus contain a poison that instantly kills anything that eats it.

African dung beetles eat animal faeces. Five thousand beetles can eat a pound of faeces in two hours.

a single female fly can hatch up to 1,000 babies (maggots) in her lifetime.

A giraffe can lick inside its own ears.

The pharaoh ant likes to live in hospitals, where it feasts on wounds, bloody bandages and IV solutions for dripping into patients' bodies.

A chicken once lived ten days after a French farmer cut its head off. He fed it with a dripper, directly into its throat.

a *lamprey* is like an eel but has no jaws. Instead, it has a sucker-like mouth with rows of teeth. It attaches itself to a fish, digs itself in, and then sucks all the fluids out of the fish, eventually killing it.

Head lice have two sharp mouthparts – one cuts through your skin and sucks up blood, the other pumps out spit containing a chemical that keeps your blood from clotting.

Cockroaches breed so fast that if all the young survived and reproduced, there would be 10 million cockroaches from a single pair by the end of a year.

Horrible Facts

A hungry shark will eat parts of its own body that have been cut off or bitten off by another animal.

Soldier flies like to lay their eggs in human faeces. The larvae (maggots) are often found in bathrooms since they crawl up the sewage pipes.

Locusts, like giant grasshoppers or crickets, travel in swarms of up to 80 million, and each eats its own weight in plants every day.

Scorpions can withstand extremes of temperature and even radiation. A scorpion could be frozen in a block of ice for three weeks and walk away unharmed and survive 200 times the dose of radiation that would kill a person!

Some leeches can suck enough blood in one meal to keep them alive for nine months.

Horn flies attack bulls – as many as 10,000 can land on a bull's back and suck its blood until it dies.

The Japanese beetle found in Canada and the USA can eat through a human eardrum.

Some types of baby Australian spider bite limbs off their mother to feed on over several weeks.

Cows partly digest the grass they eat, then vomit it back up into their mouths and chew and swallow it all over again. That's what they're doing when you see them chewing in a field when they're not munching on a fresh mouthful of grass.

The female hissing cockroach surrounds her eggs with a frothy substance that hardens; she then carries them inside her body for two weeks until they hatch.

The rattle on a rattlesnake's tail is made of rings of dead skin. It builds up as the snake grows older, so the louder the rattle the larger the snake.

Horrible Facts

An elephant's trunk is so handy that it can pluck a single blade of grass from the ground.

If one vampire bat is too ill to leave the cave, another will drink blood all night, then come home and vomit it up for the sick bat so it doesn't miss out on a meal.

The *butcherbird*, or *shrike*, impales mice, small birds and lizards on to spikes to hold them still while it eats them.

South American cane toads have special glands behind their eyes that ooze poison out of their skin. They can even shoot the poison up to 30 centimetres (nearly a foot) to deter animals that might want to eat them.

Cockroaches have an oily coating to make them slithery.

There are over 3,000 different types of mosquito and they live all over the world, even in the coldest places near the North and South poles.

aardvarks and anteaters enjoy nothing
better than slurping up ants and
termites with their long, sticky tongues.

If you're attacked by a moray eel, the only way
to get it off is to kill it, cut the head off and
break the jaws. It won't let go while it's alive.

ajellyfish excretes faeces through its
mouth – it has only one opening and
uses it for all purposes.

Flies have 1,500 tiny taste hairs on their feet
so that they can taste what they are standing
on. Ingenious!

inuit people have to cover all exposed
skin with a thick layer of mud to avoid
fierce biting flies in the summer.

Astarfish can turn its stomach inside out,
pushing it out through its mouth opening.

Driver ants and army ants both march in massive colonies and will strip to the bones any animal they come across. They'll even tackle a wounded crocodile or lion that can't get away. Driver ants slash at their victims who eventually bleed to death from thousands of tiny cuts.

You can cut a leech in half while it is feeding and it will keep on sucking, the blood spurting out of the cut end of its body.

A flea can jump up to 220 times its own body length – a flea the size of an adult human could jump over a 25-storey building and more than 0.4 kilometres (a quarter of a mile) along the ground.

The armadillo produces so much spit that it has a special reservoir to store it in.

A grotesque frog which can turn from green to beige, often lives in letterboxes and toilet cisterns in Australia and New Guinea.

Fossilized cockroaches that are 300 million years old have been found. This means they were around 100 million years before the dinosaurs evolved!

Rats that hibernate together sometimes get their tails tied up in a knot. If they urinate over themselves in the winter, they can freeze together in a block. A knot of rats is called a king rat.

When a turtle (which is immune to jellyfish stings) eats a Portuguese man-of-war jellyfish, it produces a smell that attracts sharks – so the jellyfish eventually gets its revenge!

Some leeches only suck the blood from dead animals.

Eye gnats are attracted to the moisture produced by your eyes and nose. In the USA, they are a common nuisance on hot summer evenings. They lay their eggs in rotting vegetable matter or animal faeces.

Termites fart out between 20 and 80 million tonnes of gas every year (not each, all together).

Flea larvae eat their parents' faeces – or each other. They're not fussy.

Scorpions sometimes eat their babies.

The horned lizard from South America shoots blood out of its eyes when it is attacked. It increases the blood pressure in its sinuses until they explode, spraying blood onto the attacker.

Octopuses sometimes remove stinging tentacles from jellyfish and use them as weapons.

When an opossum is threatened, it plays dead – it lies still, its tongue hanging out, excretes faeces on itself and oozes green slime that smells of rotting flesh.

The African clawed toad lays up to 10,000 eggs, but many of its tadpoles are deformed. The parents eat the deformed ones when they hatch.

A flea can jump 30,000 times without stopping.

Cockroaches can make themselves super-slim, and can flatten their bodies to a size just a little thicker than a piece of paper to crawl into cracks.

A *praying mantis* is an insect rather like a cricket, but up to 12 centimetres (5 inches) long. It can kill and eat small lizards and birds, holding them impaled on a special spike it has developed for the purpose. A really hungry mantis will eat its own babies.

The hagfish produces slimy mucus from pores in its body. If something disturbs it, it throws out strings of mucus which makes the sea around it jelly-like, gunky and impossible to swim through. They can suffocate on their own slime if they overdo it.

When a large batch of mosquito eggs hatches all at once, the babies might all attack the same unfortunate animal wandering past. They can suck it dry and kill it, if it's a small animal and there are enough mosquitoes.

The *echidna* is a mammal that lays an egg and keeps it in a pouch on its stomach. The pouch grows just before the female produces the egg and disappears again after the baby has left it.

The eyes of a chameleon can move separately, so it can look in two directions at once.

The deep-sea anglerfish can stretch its stomach to swallow prey much larger than itself.

Three-toed sloths move so slowly that algae often grows on their fur.

If a barracuda fish falls ill, it eats things that will make its flesh poisonous. That way, anything that eats it after it dies will be poisoned.

he babies of the Surinam toad grow under the mother's skin on her back. They stay there for up to 130 days.

ewly discovered monster of the deep, *Dakosaurus*, **was 4 metres (almost 14 feet) long, and had a head like a meat-eating dinosaur but the flippers and tail of a fish. Luckily, the terrifying creature died out 135 million years ago!**

he embryos of tiger sharks fight each other in the womb, the strongest killing and eating the others so that only one is ever born.

ome types of botflies lay their eggs on the abdomen of another blood-sucking insect such as a flea or tick. The eggs hatch while the host feeds the larvae and burrows into the skin of the animal it's sucking on.

History

FaCTs

Vikings used rancid butter to style and dress their hair.

In Anglo-Saxon times, shepherds were given 12 days' worth of cow manure at Christmas.

During the 900 days of the siege of Leningrad in the Second World War, 1,500 people were accused of cannibalism.

Biological warfare has been used since 600BC, when the Greek city Cirrha was besieged by Solon. He poisoned the water supply with hellebore roots and stormed the city while the citizens had diarrhoea.

in France in the late 1600s, it was considered a great honour to talk to King Louis XIV while he was on the lavatory. How intimate!

Theban king Mithradites (132–63BC) took small doses of poison regularly to develop immunity and protect himself from poisoners. When he later wanted to kill himself, the poison he took did not kill him.

a fter a massacre carried out by Indian soldiers in 1857, the British soldiers made the Indians clean up the blood – and those who refused had to lick it up.

s laves sometimes had to fight to the death in a Roman arena. To make sure they weren't just pretending to be dead, they could be prodded with a red-hot poker and hit on the head with a huge hammer.

T he Greeks played the game *knucklebones* with real bones from the knuckles of animals that have cloven feet – such as pigs, goats and antelopes.

I n Palestine 8000–9,000 years ago, a dead relative was buried under the floor of the family's house – except the head. The flesh and brain were removed from the head and the skull used as the base for a plaster mould of the person's head, which was decorated and kept.

i nuit people used to make trousers out of the *gullet* (windpipe) of a seal or walrus, using one for each leg.

Wig makers suffered during times of plague because people thought the disease could be caught from wigs made of human hair. So many second-hand wigs were infested with fleas that they were probably right!

In Sparta, Greece, in 600BC a law required that a child born imperfect – disabled or deformed – should be killed.

Toad eaters were people employed by men selling medicine at fairs and markets. The toad eater had to swallow a toad – supposed to be deadly poisonous – and then take the medicine. Their survival encouraged people to buy the medicine. They may or may not have actually swallowed the toads…

In ancient Egypt, women kept a cone of grease on their head. During the day, it melted in the hot sun and dripped down, making their hair gleam with grease.

Birching was allowed as a punishment in Britain until the 1940s. It consisted of being beaten on the bare buttocks with a bunch of twigs. Ouch!

Victorian child chimney sweeps sometimes had to crawl through chimneys as narrow as 18 centimetres (7 inches). If they didn't move quickly enough, their bare feet were pricked with burning straws.

Mary Stuart, queen of England from 1553 to 1558, had 274 people burned at the stake just for being Protestant Christians.

in 1856, the USA passed a law saying that its citizens could claim any uninhabited island anywhere in the world if it contained large deposits of bird faeces.

In the 1890s, fashionable women in Europe who wanted to look thin wore corsets laced so tightly that their ribs were sometimes broken!

During the Great Plague that struck England in 1665–66, boys at Eton school were punished for not smoking – smoking was thought to protect them from the disease.

In the 19th century, a school headmaster in York, England, massacred his pupils and hid their bodies in cupboards.

Before written or computerized records helped us to keep track of criminals, many countries marked criminals with a tattoo or a branding iron – a red-hot iron used to burn a pattern, letter or picture into their skin. This meant that everyone could see what they had done.

Bird faeces called guano were collected and sold from Peru, Chile and Bolivia for hundreds of years. It was used as a fertilizer for plants.

Mongol leader Tamerlane the Great (1336–1405) executed anyone who told him a joke he had already heard.

The Greek emperor Draco died when he was smothered by the hats and cloaks that admirers threw over him at a party. Pope Clement VII tried eating a *death cap* toadstool in 1534; it killed him.

A common way of attacking a besieged castle or city in the Middle Ages was to catapult dead animals, corpses or even the heads of enemies over the walls.

It took over two months to make an Egyptian mummy. After removing the internal organs and brain, the body was covered with a kind of salt for two months to dry out, then treated with resin, packed with sand and sawdust and wrapped in bandages.

In 2350BC the Mesopotamian king Urukagina demanded that thieves be stoned to death with stones carved with their crime.

Roman prisoners condemned to fight to death with each other or wild animals often tried to kill themselves before the fight. One man pushed a wooden spike down his throat – it was used for holding the sponge people cleaned themselves with in the lavatory.

anglo-Saxon peasants sometimes wove clothes made out of dried stinging nettles.

Anyone who rebelled against the Mesopotamian king Ashurnasirpal could expect to be skinned or buried alive. We know this because he buried some rebels inside a column and carved the story of their crime on the outside.

in ancient Rome, vestal virgins were young girls who served in a temple and could not be touched. If they committed a crime their punishment was to be buried alive since it could be done without anyone touching them.

The Romans had criminals torn apart by wild animals while the public watched. Dogs or lions were most often used, but sometimes more exotic animals were brought in.

in the time of King Charles II of England, who reigned from 1649 to 1685, dead people had to be buried in a shroud of wool, to boost business for the wool trade.

In Anglo-Saxon England, people who died in a famine were eaten by their neighbours!

The Roman king Tarquin crucified anyone who committed suicide – even though they were already dead – to show other people what would happen to their bodies if they did the same.

In 1740, a cow was found guilty of witchcraft, and hanged.

a medieval trial of guilt required a suspected criminal to plunge his or her hand into a pan of hot water and take out a stone, or carry a red-hot iron bar. The injured arm was bandaged and inspected after three days. If it was healed the person was considered innocent. If not, they were guilty and were punished.

The scarab beetle was treated as holy by the ancient Egyptians. Scarab beetles roll themselves in a ball of faeces and lay their eggs in it.

in 167BC, a Roman commander had a group of soldiers trampled to death by elephants for deserting (running away from battle).

The Mongolian ruler Ghengis Khan imposed the death penalty for urinating in water because water was so precious in the Mongolian desert.

Lord Nelson (1758–1805) admiral of the English fleet, slept in a coffin in his cabin. The coffin was made from the mast of an enemy French ship.

The Spanish Inquisition was set up to find people who committed crimes against the church and its teachings. They often questioned and tortured people until they confessed. In the case of a child under 10, though, they could go straight to the torture and not even bother with the questions.

in India, people used to believe that the eyes from a slow lorris – a nocturnal creature like a monkey with no tail – could work as a love potion.

During the time of Henry VIII of England, who reigned from 1508 to 1547, the punishment for poisoners was to be boiled alive.

To make violin strings, the gut of a sheep – which could be 30 metres (over 98 feet) long – was removed intact.

The blood, flesh and fat were then scraped off the outside, the half-digested grass was squeezed out and it was washed out carefully. The wider end was used as sausage skins, the rest for violin strings.

The Roman emperor Valerian was captured by visigoths (a barbaric tribe) invading Rome in AD260, who skinned him alive and then displayed the skin as a sign of their triumph.

Ancient Greeks used to blow up a pig's bladder like a balloon and use it as a ball.

an Anglo-Saxon cure for baldness was to rub the ash from burned bees into the head.

Soldiers fighting in the trenches in the First World War often suffered from trench foot (spending too long in cold, wet trenches made their feet rot). Some had to have their feet amputated because of it.

a **French medieval torture involved trapping a person in the stocks – a wooden structure that held their ankles while they sat on the ground – pouring salt water over their bare feet and letting a goat lick it off.**

When Sir Walter Ralegh was executed in 1618, his wife had his head embalmed. She carried it around with her for 29 years, until her own death.

The servants of a dead Egyptian pharaoh were often killed and buried with him or sealed alive in his pyramid.

Wool used to be softened by people trampling on it in a large vat of stale (two week-old) urine and ground clay. The people who did this were called 'fullers'.

The Hungarian countess Elizabeth Bathori killed more than 600 young girls in the 1500s in order to drink and bathe in their blood.

A Saxon cure for madness was a beating with a whip made from the skin of a dolphin.

ancient Egyptians sometimes brought a mummified body to banquets to remind diners that one day they would die.

Monks in Sicily mummified dead bodies until 1920. A display of 6,000 can be seen in catacombs in Palermo, standing around or lying on shelves.

Hanging, drawing, and quartering was a punishment for the worst crimes in England from 1241. First the prisoner was nearly strangled by hanging, then cut open, had his innards removed and cooked in front of him, and finally was chopped into four pieces. By the mid-1700s, prisoners were killed before the drawing and quartering.

Early colonists in America used to clean their windows with rags dipped in urine. In the Middle Ages, butchers often killed animals for meat in their shops, then threw the innards out into the street.

Romans who killed a relative would be executed by being tied in a sack with a live dog, cockerel, snake and monkey and thrown into a river.

A dead body found in the Alps in 1991 was at first thought to be a climber who had died. Investigators discovered it was a man who had been mummified naturally in the ice after dying 5,300 years ago. They named him Otzi. So many people associated with the discovery of Otzi have died young that some believe the mummy is cursed.

Fashionable women in Japan and Vietnam stained their teeth black until the mid-1900s.

The poet Shelley drowned off the coast of Italy in 1822. His body was washed up, half eaten by fish, and cremated on the beach by his friends. One of them cut his heart from the burnt body and gave it to Shelley's wife who kept it all her life.

The Incas of South America used to mummify their dead kings and leave them sitting on their thrones.

During a famine and drought in Jamestown, America, in 1609, one settler was executed for eating his dead wife.

People hunting animals examine the faeces of their quarry to find out information about the size, sex and type of animal. In the Middle Ages, hunters often carried the faeces around with them while they hunted, storing them in their hunting horn.

Queen Christina of Sweden, who reigned from 1640 to 1654, had a miniature cannon and crossbow for executing fleas.

in the 1700s, people wore huge hairstyles made of a mixture of real hair and horse hair or other fibres. Since they rarely cleaned them – keeping them in place for months on end – they carried sticks to knock vermin out of their hairstyles.

Sailors in the olden days often had a single gold tooth, which could be pulled out and used to pay for their funeral if they died away from home.

French actress Sarah Bernhardt took a coffin with her on all her travels. She learned her lines while lying in the coffin and even entertained her lovers in it.

An Egyptian mummy can have more than 20 layers of bandages, with glue between the layers. Every finger and toe was carefully wrapped separately. It took 15 days to wrap a royal mummy.

ancient Romans made hair dye from pigeon faeces.

Uruguay's rugby team was stranded in the Andes in South America after a plane crash in 1979. It took 70 days for them to be rescued, and they had to eat the other passengers who had died in the crash.

an ancient Egyptian who was feeling a bit unwell might eat a mixture of mashed mouse and faeces. Mmmmmmm, bound to make you feel better!

In 1846, 87 pioneers crossing the mountains of Nevada, USA, became trapped in bad weather. By the end of the winter, 40 of them had been eaten by the others.

in the 1700s, European women had their gums pierced so that they could fit hooks to hold their false teeth in place.

King Pepi II of Egypt had himself surrounded by naked slaves smeared with honey so that any biting flies would be attracted to them and not bite him.

in the 1800s, flea circuses were popular – the fleas were glued into costumes and stuck to wires or each other to look as though they were performing tricks.

Ivan the Terrible blinded the two architects who designed his new church of Saint Basil's so that they could never make anything more beautiful.

The Russian ruler Peter the Great had his wife's lover decapitated and insisted that she keep his head in a jar of alcohol beside her bed as a reminder of her crime.

Mongolian leader Tamerlane played polo using the skulls of enemies killed in battle.

in the Middle Ages, people made washing powder from wood ash and urine.

In China, in the 1500s, a common method of committing suicide was by eating a pound of salt. Nasty!

The word 'thug' comes from 'thuggees', who were an Indian cult – sometimes described as the world's first mafia – who used to trick and murder people to use them as human sacrifices to their goddess Kali.

In the 1600s and later, Egyptian mummies were ground up to use in medicines around Europe.

Vlad the Impaler, ruler of Transylvania, had over 20,000 enemies impaled on spikes between 1456 and 1476.

British king James I's tongue was too large for his mouth so he slobbered all the time and was a very messy eater.

Charles I was executed by beheading, but had his head sewn back on so that his family could pay their respects to his body. His doctor stole a bone from his neck and had it made into a salt cellar.

A Bohemian army general was so devoted to his country that when he died he asked for his skin to be removed and made into a drum that could be beaten in defiance of Bohemia's enemies. It was used nearly 200 years later at the start of the Thirty Years' War in 1618.

i n the 1700s, fashionable European women commonly shaved off their real eyebrows and stuck on false ones made from mouse fur.

L ondon prisoners condemned to death used to go to chapel on the Sunday before their execution where they had to sit around a coffin while the priest told them how sinful they were.

i n times of famine, Stone Age tribes would eat old women before dogs – they thought them less useful.

T he body tag from the corpse of Lee Harvey Oswald, who shot President John F. Kennedy, was sold for £3,600 ($5,300) at an auction.

James, Duke of Monmouth, was beheaded in 1685 but when it was discovered that there was no official portrait of him, his head was stitched back on and he posed for his portrait at last.

In 1981, 300 people thrown into the water in a ferry accident in Brazil were eaten alive by piranhas.

The 15th-century German king Wenceslas was so angry with his chef after a particularly bad meal that he had him roasted alive.

Saint Ignatius of Antioch prayed to be eaten by wild animals; when the Roman emperor Trajan sentenced him to be eaten by lions in AD110 he fell to his knees and thanked him.

In 896, the rotting body of Pope Formosus was removed from his coffin, dressed in his papal robes and put on trial. Found guilty, his blessing finger was cut off and he was thrown in the river.

The body of British philosopher Jeremy Bentham was preserved and kept in an open wooden box which is still on display at University College, London. For many years, Bentham was brought out to attend special functions and meetings.

Roman gladiator and slave rebel leader Spartacus had 300 of his followers crucified to show the others what would happen to them if they deserted his army.

During the Reign of Terror following the French Revolution, 17,000 people were beheaded using the guillotine.

Scottish bagpipes were originally made from the entire skin or stomach of a dead sheep.

Russian leader Peter the Great had a museum in which he kept the stuffed bodies of deformed people and animals, such as a child with two heads and a sheep with five feet. The museum was looked after by a deformed dwarf who knew that he would become an exhibit when he died.

it took the executioner three blows to behead Mary Queen of Scots in 1567. And he still had to saw through the remaining skin and gristle with a knife.

In ancient Egypt, a flea catcher would cover himself in milk and stand in the middle of the flea-infested room until all the fleas jumped onto him then he'd leave, taking them all with him.

english hatmakers used to soften the straw they plaited into hats by spitting on it.

Houses in many parts of the world have been made from a mixture called *wattle and daub* – horse manure and straw.

During witchcraft trials in Salem, Massachusetts, USA, in 1692, 25 people were condemned to death on the flimsy evidence of a group of hysterical girls.

King Kokodo of the Congo ruled for three years after his death. His body was wheeled around in a box during this part of his reign…

Leather used to be cured with a mixture of dog and chicken faeces smeared on it for many months. The fat and rotting meat scraps were scraped off with a knife.

It is said that the cursed mummy of Egyptian princess Amen-Ra was on board the *Titanic* when it sank in 1912, killing 1,500 people. The mummy was being sent from the British Museum to the USA; only the lid of the mummy's coffin is still in the British Museum.

Bald Romans used to make a paste of mashed up flies and spread it over their heads in the belief that it would make their hair regrow. It didn't...

Ivan the Terrible of Russia punished a bishop by having him stitched into the skin of a dead bear and releasing a pack of hounds to hunt and kill him.

Instead of a hollow pumpkin with a candle inside, Celtic people are said to have used real human heads cut from defeated enemies to keep away ghosts and ghouls in the autumn.

Chimney sweeps used to have three baths a year – one in the spring, one in the autumn and one for Christmas. The rest of the time, they were covered in soot.

In the past, European women sometimes wore a tube filled with sticky tree sap around their necks or on animal fur. These tubes were supposed to attract and trap any fleas on their bodies.

The earliest cosmetic surgery was practised by doctors in India who made fake noses for criminals whose noses had been cut off as a punishment for their crimes.

If sheep grazed on pastures full of clover, shepherds sometimes had to puncture the animals' stomachs with a sharp knife to release all the gases that had built up inside them.

In the old days, a *whipping boy* used to sit next to a prince in lessons. If the prince made a mistake, or did something wrong, the whipping boy was punished instead of the prince.

In the Middle Ages a royal farter was employed to jump around farting in front of the king to amuse him.

In Africa, it was common to bend back springy saplings and tie them beneath the ears of omeone about to be beheaded, so that the person's last sensation would be of their head flying through the air.

Until 1868, criminals could be transported from England and sent to Australia for 7–14 years for even petty crimes. The youngest victim was a boy of nine, who was transported for stealing.

King Henry VIII of England, used the death penalty more than any other English king in history.

a punishment used in China in the old days was for a prisoner to be kept in an iron cage with his head sticking out the top. The cage was too tall to sit in, and too short to stand up. Some prisoners were left to starve to death inside.

A common test for the guilt of a person accused of witchcraft was to throw them in a pond. If they floated, they were guilty and were executed. If they sank, they were innocent – but probably drowned.

a t banquets, the Gauls used to award the legs of roast animals to the bravest warriors. Sometimes fights to the death resulted from the squabbles over who should get them.

L ong ago, criminals would be hanged in a metal cage called a *gibbet*, or in chains, near the scene of their crime and left there 'until their bones rotted to nothing'.

In 1577, an outbreak of typhus in a jail in Oxford, England, killed 300 people – the judges, jury, witnesses and spectators at criminal trials. The prisoners, used to living in filthy conditions, all survived.

Vlad the Impaler used to entertain guests to dinner surrounded by the bodies of people he had executed, impaled on spikes.

During the French Revolution, large crowds watched public executions by guillotine and people would rush forward to try to collect blood dripping from the heads lifted to show the crowd. They would keep bloody handkerchiefs as souvenirs of the outing.

In 1857, a group of Indian people who rebelled against the ruling British were strapped across the mouths of live cannons and blown to bits when cannonballs were shot through them.

People who killed themselves used to be buried at a crossroads with a stake through their heart. It was thought that they couldn't go to heaven, and the crossroads would confuse their ghost so that it couldn't find the way home to haunt anyone.

A trusted servant of William of Orange, a Dutch king of England, spent money the king had given him for clothes on pistols, which he used to shoot the king. As punishment, he had his flesh pulled off with red-hot pincers, his guts pulled out and his body cut into pieces.

in 1685, a wolf that terrorized a village near Ansbach in Germany was sentenced to be dressed in human clothing and hanged.

The first person to be found guilty of a crime on the basis of fingerprint evidence was an Argentinian woman who murdered her children in 1892. Her fingerprints were found in blood on a door frame.

in ancient **Babylon, a doctor who accidentally killed a patient had his hands cut off.**

A punishment for an English woman who nagged her husband or gossiped too much was to wear a metal cage over her head called a *scold's bridle*. It had a spiked plate inside her mouth that would cut her tongue if she moved it to speak.

inca women washed their hair in week-old urine, braided it, and then used more old urine to keep it in place.

The Chinchorro people of Chile mummified their dead 8,000 years ago. They cut off the arms and legs, removed and smoked the skin, strapped sticks to the bones and replaced all the soft parts with grass and ashes, then put the whole body back together and painted it.

During excavations at a circle of standing stones in **Avebury, England,** in 1938, archaeologists found the body of a man who had been crushed under a falling stone in the 1320s when villagers had tried to bury the stones.

Over 100,000 people have been tried for witchcraft in Europe since 1100, most of them tortured and eventually executed.

it is reported that during **Napoleon's** invasion of **Russia** in 1812 some soldiers cut open dead horses and sheltered inside them to avoid freezing to death.

English revolutionary Oliver Cromwell died of natural causes, but opponents had his body dug up, tried and executed. His head is kept in an unmarked location in Sidney Sussex College, Cambridge.

Some **Stone Age people** believed the spirit could only escape when the flesh had gone from the body, so they left corpses to rot or be eaten by wild animals, or hacked off the flesh, before burying them.

As well as people, the ancient Egyptians mummified all kinds of animals including cats, crocodiles, birds – even fish and beetles.

at the **Aztec festival celebrating** *Xipe Totec* – the **Aztec god of spring** – prisoners of war were flayed alive. Their skins were then worn ceremonially by priests to represent the renewal of earth and the start of new life in spring.

People of the North American Sioux tribe used to make an amulet of their own, dried umbilical cord – the cord that connects the unborn baby to its mother's body – which they thought guaranteed a long life.

a **1,000-year-old grave in England was found to contain a rich woman in a coffin beneath a poor woman pinned down by a big stone. She was probably a slave, buried alive to serve the rich woman in the afterlife.**

The ancient Britons used to practise euthanasia by jumping off cliffs to their deaths. If individuals were too elderly to jump they would be pushed!

in the 1700s, the penalty for wearing tartan or playing the bagpipes in Britain was death.

Anglo-Saxon parents were allowed to sell children up to the age of seven to be slaves 'if they needed to do so'.

an lhasa apso dog was once imprisoned and kept on death row in a prison in Washington State, USA, for over eight years for biting.

For nearly 1,000 years, Chinese women had their feet bound to keep them small. The toes were bent underneath, breaking all the bones, and the feet were kept tightly bandaged from childhood until death. The practice was banned in 1911.

apart from the heart, an Egyptian mummy doesn't have any internal organs left inside the body. The others were removed and put into separate canopic jars that were buried with it.

British schools used to keep at least two types of standard cane for hitting naughty children. Children over 15 years of age could be hit with the senior cane, which was longer and thicker than that used on younger children.

people used to believe that smearing their clothes with fat from a dead pig would keep away fleas.

Horrible Facts

The Jivaros in the Andes shrunk the heads of enemies killed in battle. They skinned the head, then stitched up the eyes and mouth and stewed the skin for a couple of hours with herbs. Then they dried it, stuffed it with hot stones and sand and polished it.

In the War of the Pacific (1879–1884), Chile fought against Bolivia and Peru over who was allowed to collect bird faeces and whether they should have to pay a tax on them.

When King Philip of Spain died in 1560, his devastated wife would not allow him to be buried, but had his coffin accompany her everywhere she went.

Before modern plumbing, a *gong scourer* was a boy who was sent into cesspits to scoop and scrape all the muck into buckets and remove it. The job was so horrible it was done at night so that people wouldn't have to see it happening.

Csar Peter III of Russia was crowned 34 years after he died. His coffin was opened so that the crown could be put on his head.

The body of William the Conqueror was too big for his coffin, so two soldiers jumped up and down on him to try to squish him in. This broke his back and made his stomach explode.

Before the days of lipstick, women used to colour their lips red with cochineal, a paste made from crushed beetles.

The law system drawn up by the Roman emperor Draco made every crime a capital offence – one for which the criminal could be executed.

In the Middle Ages, the boys who looked after dogs used for hunting had to sleep in the kennels with them.

Before the invention of real footballs, kids used to stuff a pig's bladder with peas to kick around.

Ancient Romans used to make themselves sick during a banquet so that they could eat more after they were full. A special slave had the job of clearing up the mess.

In England, suicide used to be illegal. The punishment for trying to kill yourself was death.

In medieval France, a cockerel that was found sitting on an egg (which only hens normally do) was found guilty of being a devil and was burned at the stake.

In 1808, Tommy Otter was hanged for killing his girlfriend. His body was left chained in a tree and a year later a pair of blue tits made a nest in his skull and reared eight chicks.

To honour the goddess Teteoinnan at the time of harvest, the Aztecs skinned a woman as a sacrifice. Her skin was then worn by a priest at a harvest festival.

in the 1800s, Mongolian prisoners were fastened into a wooden box little larger than a coffin where they were left to die. Some were given food for years, but never allowed out.

In the 1800s, there were several cases of people being buried when they were not really dead. Terrible stories about opened coffins with scratch marks on the inside, and corpses with fingernails worn away by trying to escape, led to cautious people being buried with a system of warning bells fitted in the coffin which they could ring if they woke up.

archaeologists in Peru have found skeletons of victims tied up and left to be eaten by vultures, perhaps as a sacrifice.

An ancient Egyptian cure for burns involved warming a frog in goat dung and applying it to the burn.

science

Facts

Many tribes around the world have practised *trepanning* since the Stone Age. It involves drilling a hole in the skull, often with a stone, to ease headaches by letting out evil spirits. People frequently survived, as many skulls have been found with several such holes, some partially healed. In 1962, a Dutch doctor decided to try trepanning. He used an electric drill to make a hole in his own head.

Malaria is a deadly disease spread by mosquitoes. It is caused by a tiny parasite that lives inside a person's blood cells. Malaria kills up to 3 million people a year.

early Indian surgeons used ants to hold the edges of wounds together. They would get an ant to bite through both sides of the wound, then twist off the ant's body and throw it away, leaving the head in place with the jaws acting as a stitch.

Railway workers in France in the 1800s claimed to have freed a pterodactyl trapped in rock. They said it flapped, squawked and died. Reports of frogs and other animals trapped in solid rock are quite common, but not scientifically proven.

Snake venom is not normally poisonous if swallowed because stomach acid alters the chemicals in it.

A toxin in the nectar of laurels and rhododendrons makes honey made from these plants poisonous. In 66BC, Roman troops were lured by their enemies into a grove where bees made honey from these flowers. The soldiers ate it and were slaughtered while sick.

The scientific name for a fear of peanut butter sticking to the roof of your mouth is *arachibutyrophobia*.

If you fell into a black hole you would be stretched into an incredibly long, thin string in a process called *spaghettification*.

Cells taken from the inside of baby teeth when they fall out have been grown and have reproduced in the laboratory. Put into the jaws of mice, they grow into soft teeth, with no hard enamel on the outside.

Urine contains chemicals that we use in cleaning fluids. In the past, urine was used for cleaning things.

Scientists investigating tumour growth added a gene from a firefly to make a glow-in-the-dark tumour. The tumour is visible through the skin of a test animal, so scientists can see if it grows or shrinks.

There are 'banks' where the umbilical cords of new babies can be stored in case future medical developments make it possible to grow new organs or tissues from cells in them.

a fear of worms is called *scoleciphobia*.

There are over 20,000 road crashes involving kangaroos in Australia every year, so a robotic, kangaroo-like crash test dummy called Robo-Roo is used to test how badly cars will be damaged.

If you cut spinach with an iron knife, both will go black as a chemical in the spinach reacts with the iron.

Some animals respond to small amounts of poisonous gas and have been used as early warning systems. German soldiers kept cats in the trenches of the First World War to smell gas, and British miners kept budgies in cages because they died quickly if gas escaped into the mine.

A person would need to weigh around 650 kilograms (1,433 pounds) to have enough fat to stop a bullet. Although their body would be bulletproof, they could still be killed by a shot to the head.

Horrible Facts

Victorian children were often given their own salt cellar, which they were told was a sign of being grown up. In fact, the salt was mixed with bromide, which made the children calmer and better behaved.

Potatoes, aubergines, tomatoes and peppers all belong to the same family of plants as deadly nightshade!

Scientists are working on a microscopic robotic tadpole to deliver medicines – the tadpole would 'swim' through the patient's blood vessels to take the medicine where it's needed.

Not all dead bodies rot. Under the right conditions, some of the fat can turn to a soap-like substance so that if the body is dug up, even years later, it can look much the same as when it was buried.

Police scientists investigating a murder can work out how long a body has been dead by looking at the kinds of maggots, worms and insects that are eating it.

archaeologists find out about what dinosaurs ate by examining fossilized dinosaur faeces called *coprolites*. They have to be soaked in water for three days first to soften them.

An unusual form of drug abuse is licking cane toads. They make a slime containing a drug that produces hallucinations (strange experiences or visions). People in some parts of Australia and the USA have started licking the toads to enjoy the drug.

Fake mermaids made from bits of monkey and fish have been produced to fool scientists for years – most recently with one claimed to have been washed up by the tsunami in Asia in 2004. the oldest so-called mummified mermaid is 1,400 years old and from Japan.

Some types of pitcher plant have long trailing stems which capture and digest small animals such as frogs.

australian Benjamin Drake Van Wissen invented machinery to mine *guano* (bird droppings) on the Pacific island of Nauru and turn it into fertilizer.

Green potatoes contain a poison, *solanin*, which can be deadly. It develops in old potatoes that are not kept in the dark. Eating 2 kilograms (4.4 pounds) of green potatoes could be fatal.

if you are trapped in snow in an avalanche, it's impossible to tell which way is up (and so which way to dig yourself out). Urinate and see which direction the yellow stain spreads – gravity will pull the urine down.

In 1822, Dr. William Beaumont studied human digestion as it happened, through a hole in the side and stomach of a patient who had been shot. The hole did not heal, allowing Dr. Beaumont to study, but also allowing food and drink to ooze out if it was not covered up.

Oil is made from the decayed bodies of animals and plants that died millions of years ago and have been squashed deep underground ever since.

In an attempt to kill malaria-carrying mosquitoes, an American scientist built towers to attract bats. He enticed them in with fabric covered with bat droppings, and played music near the bats' old homes to drive them out. After a few years, malaria infection dropped from 89 per cent of the population to zero.

In 1999, an artist in Chicago, USA, announced his plan to grow a glow-in-the-dark dog by adding a gene from jellyfish to it.

During the First World War, goldfish were used to check whether all traces of poisonous gas had been washed out of gas masks. The mask was rinsed and filled with water, then a goldfish was dropped in. If it died, there was still gas left in it.

The most poisonous metal in the world is arsenic. It used to be made into flypaper for killing flies, but it killed some people, too.

People used to use white lead powder to make their skin look white and beautiful, but it gave them lead poisoning and slowly killed them. As their skin looked worse once the poison took effect, they used more white lead to cover up the damage.

around 1,400 years ago, the Chinese used to make gunpowder by boiling up and burning pig manure. To make sure it was ready, and not polluted with salt, they licked the crystals.

It can take 100 years for the body of a whale at the bottom of the sea to disappear completely, as it is slowly eaten away by different animals, plants and microbes.

a small animal such as a mouse can be dropped 1,000 metres (3,280 feet) down a mine shaft and suffer no harm because the fastest speed it can fall it is not enough to crush its body. The larger an animal or object, the shorter the distance it can safely fall.

Our blood is red because it uses an iron compound to carry oxygen – some spiders have blue blood because theirs uses a copper compound instead.

John Haigh killed six people in London, UK, in the 1940s, dissolving their bodies in a bath of acid, hoping he could wash away all the evidence. However, on finding three human gallstones and a pair of dentures belonging to one of his victims in the sludge left behind, the police had enough evidence to convict him.

Old cannonballs brought up from the seabed can explode and kill divers. Bacteria eat away part of the metal, producing gases that rapidly expand when the cannonballs come to the surface.

Scraping mould off your food doesn't get rid of it – behind the fuzzy part you can see, mould strings extend into the food up to nine times the length of the visible part.

If you draw pictures in the condensation on a window, the picture will reappear next time the window mists over as a layer of grease from your skin stays on the glass and repels the water.

earthworms bring 4 million kilograms (8.8 million pounds) of earth to the surface on every square kilometre (0.38 square miles) of open ground each year.

In the 1600s, spiders rolled in butter were recommended as a cure for malaria.

There have been several recorded cases of spontaneous human combustion (people who apparently burst into flames for no good reason). Sometimes, all that is left is a burnt patch and perhaps a foot or some singed clothing.

A medieval cure for stammering was scalding the tongue with a red-hot iron. Unsurprisingly, it didn't work…

Rats trained to look for land mines are so light that they don't trigger the mechanism if they tread on one. Instead, they scratch and bite at the ground when they smell explosives, and the handler deals with the mine.

If you fall off a very high cliff or building, the fastest speed you will ever fall at is around 200 kilometres (124 miles) per hour. This is called *terminal velocity*, and it's enough to make a nasty splat.

Bird droppings are the main export of the island Nauru in the western Pacific Ocean. They're used for fertilizer, as they're rich in nitrogen.

Horses killed in the First World War were recycled as explosives – their fat was boiled down to be used in making TNT.

Scientists believe that all vertebrates (animals with backbones) evolved from giant tadpoles measuring 6 centimetres (2.5 inches) long, that swam around 550 million years ago.

Some wealthy people have their bodies *cryopreserved* (deep-frozen) when they die, in the hope that in the future someone will find a cure for their cause of death and resurrect them. The popular urban legend that Walt Disney was cryopreserved is false; he was cremated.

If potatoes were discovered today, they would probably be banned under European Union regulations for being too dangerous.

The chemical *phosphorous* was discovered by German chemist Hening Brandt in 1669. He made it by leaving urine to rot and then heating it until the liquid evaporated.

Hungry huskies and polar bears have been known to attack explorers when they urinate – they are attracted by the smell.

It is so cold in space, that urine flushed out of a spacecraft instantly freezes into a stream of yellow crystals.

There are 100 million times more insects than people on Earth and their total weight is 12 times the total weight of people.

In an emergency, coconut milk can be used as substitute for the watery part of blood in a blood transfusion.

Japanese scientists have managed to grow tadpole eyes from scratch in the laboratory. They transplanted the eyes into tadpoles. The eyes worked even after the tadpoles changed into frogs.

The average bed is home to 6 million dust mites. Lined up neatly, 10,000 bacteria would stretch across your thumbnail.

ergot is a fungus that grows on rye and causes people to act crazy if they eat it. Some historians believe that people who were accused of witchcraft and said they could fly, or those who accused others of displaying strange, magical behaviour, may have had ergot poisoning.

The Masai tribe in Africa drink cow or bull urine as a sedative (drug to calm people down or make them sleepy).

There is a cockroach museum in Plano, Texas.

The largest living thing in the world is a fungus in Washington state, USA, which covers 6.5 square kilometres (2.5 square miles) and has been growing for hundreds of years.

The germs present in faeces can pass through 10 layers of toilet paper – that's why you need to wash your hands!

Some people – most of them in the USA – claim that they have been abducted by aliens from space while they slept, had their bodies experimented on and sometimes their minds changed, and were then returned to Earth.

a *will-o'-the-wisp* **is a flame of burning marsh gas that appears in boggy areas at night. It has lured many travellers to a muddy death when they have left the path to follow it, believing it to be someone with a light.**

The castor bean plant contains the most deadly poison in the natural world, *ricin*. Just 70 micrograms (2-millionths of an ounce) could kill an adult human. It is 12,000 times more poisonous than rattlesnake venom!

i **t's been suggested that Americans' bodies decompose much more slowly than they used to because they eat so many preservatives in their foods.**

Some scientists think that being too clean might make us ill – some studies suggest that people need to eat a small amount of dirt in order to kick start their immune systems. Not learning to fight infections can lead to asthma and other allergic problems.

One possible way of controlling cockroaches being explored in the USA is to release parasitic worms that will kill the roaches but don't harm people.

The *stinking corpse plant*, or *rafflesia*, is a huge parasitic flower that smells like rotting meat. The flower is up to a metre (about 3 feet) across and is the largest flower in the world. It grows directly out of a creeping vine, from which it gains all its nourishment without ever growing leaves of its own.

Scientists working on transplant techniques grew a human ear on the back of a mouse. The ear is moulded using human cartilage cells, and nourished by the mouse's blood as it grows.

he average glass of London tap water has passed through nine people's bladders before it reaches your sink.

eodorants don't stop you sweating but they kill the bacteria that make sweat smell.

he earliest study of brain damage was of railway worker Phineas Gage. In 1848, an explosion shot a thick iron rod through his head. Although he recovered physically, his character changed completely. His skull and the iron rod are on display at Harvard University, USA.

cure for whooping cough used in Yorkshire, England in the 1800s was to drink a bowl of soup with nine frogs hidden in it. You couldn't make it yourself – it only worked if you didn't know about the frogs. (And probably not then, either!)

omans dressed small wounds with spiderwebs soaked in vinegar.

a Roman cure for *epilepsy* (having fits) was to take a bath in the blood of a gladiator.

P eople on the Pacific island of Chuuk use a love potion made from centipede's teeth and stingray tails.

F or centuries, it was illegal to cut up dead bodies, so surgeons and scientists had to pay criminals to steal the corpses of executed prisoners from the gallows in order to learn about anatomy.

A n old cure for tuberculosis consisted of cutting open a newly dead cow, pulling the folds of skin around your neck and breathing in deeply. Smelly!

a chemical extracted from leeches is used as a painkiller.

A ir-conditioning systems are home to lots of nasty bacteria. And because they pump the same air around a building again and again, they are one of the best ways of spreading diseases to everyone in the building.

electric bug zappers splatter dead bugs around the room as they are vaporized by the lethal electric current.

the Australian 1991 Inventor of the Year Award was won by the designer of a cockroach zapper. The roach is lured into a trap with food, then electrocuted.

if you flush the toilet without putting the seat down, a fine aerosol spray of urine and faeces flies into the air of the bathroom – and some lands on your toothbrush. Gross!

A stinging tree in Australia can cause intense pain and even death. Tiny hairs full of poison break off the leaves and stick to the skin, which can then heal over the injury, trapping the poison inside. Even standing near the tree can cause painful nosebleeds!

a medieval cure for meningitis involved splitting a pigeon in two and laying the two halves, cut side down, on the patient's head.

An old cure for a headache involved tying the rope used to hang a criminal around your temples.

a common cure for all kinds of illnesses in the past was 'bleeding' the patient. This could be done by the doctor making a small cut and putting a hot cup over the wound to suck out blood, or by putting bloodsucking leeches on the skin. Using leeches is being reintroduced by some Western doctors.

In England in the 1500s, horse urine was rubbed into the scalp as a cure for baldness.

To catch the leeches for medical use, volunteers stand in rivers until the leeches attach themselves to their skin.

Atreatment for the skin disease *psoriasis* available in Turkey involves sitting in a bath full of live fish, which eat away all the flaking skin.

in the late 1800s, the Egyptian railways were fuelled by burning ancient mummies because they were more plentiful than coal and wood.

The Venus flytrap is a plant with fleshy traps that look rather like a clam, edged with spikes. If an insect lands on the trap, the halves snap shut, trapping it, and then juices from the plant dissolve the insect for the plant to absorb.

To investigate what owls eat, scientists take apart *owl pellets* (owl faeces) and piece together the bones and fur from different creatures the owl has eaten.

One of the best ways of cleaning an infected wound, used before the days of antibiotics and now with infections that antibiotics can't treat, is to put maggots into it to eat all the rotting flesh.

Sundew plants have lots of sticky tentacles. When an insect lands on them, it can't escape and the glue on the plant digests the insect's body, feeding the plant.

In 1986, 92 people were killed in Bangladesh by giant hailstones weighing up to 1 kilogram (2 pounds 3 ounces) each.

Sometimes frozen blocks of toilet waste flushed from aeroplanes fall to earth.

The scientific name for fear of slime is *blennophobia*. Who knew!

The English rhyme 'Ring-a-Ring-o'-Roses' dates from the time of the bubonic plague. The 'roses' refer to red spots that appeared before boils started, the 'posies' to flowers people carried around to counteract the bad air that they thought caused plague, and the sneezing was an early symptom.

In the Middle Ages, people thought they could cure the medical condition *rheumatism* by carrying a dead shrew in their pockets.

The Fore people of Papua New Guinea traditionally eat the bodies of their dead relatives, including the brain. During the 1950s and 1960s an outbreak of the disease *kuru* was traced to the practice and people were dissuaded from enjoying the usual funeral meal.

Scientists are working on a design for a spacecraft that will be partly fuelled by burning astronauts' faeces.

Some babies are born still enclosed in the sac that holds the fluid in which they develop in the womb. It used to be considered a sign of good luck. Second World War leader Winston Churchill was born like this.

In the 19th century, arsenic was often used to create green colouring. A cake with green icing, coloured with arsenic, killed children who ate it at a birthday party, prompting chemists to ask for laws about what could be used in foods.

a new design for a rat trap sends a text message to a pest controller when it kills a rat, so that the rat can be quickly removed before it starts to decompose and smell.

S ometimes fish or frogs fall from the sky like rain – and there have been cases of a shower of meat and a rain of maggots.

T aking a bath in the water used to wash a corpse was thought be another way to cure epilepsy.

U sing genetic engineering techniques, scientists have a made a mouse that glows in the dark.

T here are about 4,000 microbes above every 6.4 square centimetres (1 square inch) of ground.

B odies buried in lead-lined coffins sometimes explode, as gases from the rotting body are held in by the strong metal. If they are dug up and opened, bits of body can burst out and fly off in all directions.

equipment retrieved from the moon in the 1970s contained germs left there in 1967 – they were still alive.

The *strangler fig* grows from a seed dropped on another tree in bird or opossum faeces. It grows roots around the host tree and shades its leaves, eventually strangling the host tree to death.

Plants aren't as harmless as they seem. There are more than 600 types of carnivorous plants – plants that eat animals or insects.

Pitcher plants have a deep funnel filled with acid that dissolves any insects or small animals that fall into it. The dead creatures are used as food by the plant.

a zookeeper in Germany tried to treat an elephant for constipation with laxative foods and an *enema* (pumping oil into its anus through a tube). His cure was effective – the elephant produced 90 kilograms (200 pounds) of faeces, which landed on the keeper and suffocated him.

Horrible Facts

A firestorm is an uncontrollable fire, often the result of a bombing raid. Temperatures can rise to 800 degrees Celsius (1,472 degrees Fahrenheit) and air is sucked into the firestorm with the force of a hurricane. People who aren't burned can suffocate.

Fat contains a huge amount of energy. Polar explorers sometimes eat hunks of greasy seal fat to build up enough calories to keep their bodies warm.

P iles of horse manure steam in cold weather because the action of bacteria breaking it down produces so much heat. The manure, filled with water and gas, is a very good insulator, so it stays hot.

In 1890, a young girl was smeared with phosphorous so that she would glow in the dark and could act as a ghost in a hoax séance. She was poisoned by the chemical and died.

Scabs are formed when chemical proteins react with special blood cells called platelets, which cause the blood to get sticky and clump together. Once you've clotted, lots of different chemicals and cells work together to dry out the clot and form a scab, keeping out germs while the cells underneath repair themselves. So, if you pick a scab you're messing with all your body's hard work!

In 2000, UK mountaineer Major Michael Lane gave a museum five of his own fingers and eight of his toes which had dropped off as a result of frostbite when he was climbing Mount Everest in 1976.

A French cement factory uses soiled nappies as fuel to heat its cement kilns.

Volcanic vents deep under the sea are home to strange plants and animals that can live in high temperatures and poisonous, acidic water.

Scientists studying Mormon crickets cut the heads off to see what the crickets had been eating – and found many had eaten other Mormon crickets.

Doctors used to test for diabetes by tasting the patient's urine – diabetes made it taste sweet because sugar was lost in it.

The first frozen chicken was created by Sir Francis Bacon who stuffed a plucked chicken with snow in 1626 to experiment with refrigeration. It worked, but he died from a chill contracted during the experiment. The chicken is said to haunt Pond Square in London.

Diamonds are so hard they are often used as the tip of a dentist's drill because they can grind through teeth.

It is possible to drown in mud – and almost impossible to save someone who is drowning in mud as so much force is needed to pull them against the weight of it.

if blue whales tried to live on land, they would be crushed and suffocated by their own weight. They can live successfully in water because it supports them.

On the east coast of the USA there is a laboratory that leaves dead bodies of humans and animals outside to decay so that scientists can study the rate at which they rot, and the different maggots and microbes that help them decompose.

in an experiment with a condemned prisoner, Doctor Beaurieux of France discovered in 1905 that a person – or head – can hear and respond for around 25 seconds after beheading.

Soap can be made by dissolving animal fat using an alkali such as sodium hydroxide. Soap used to be made from sheep or pig fat.

Occasionally, babies are born with a full set of teeth.

Honey kills germs. Spreading it on wounds can stop them becoming infected.

Most bacteria are only about 0.00025 of a centimetre (0.0001 of an inch) across. But monster bacteria have been found at the bottom of the ocean off the coast of Africa. They are so big they can be seen without a microscope – they're each about the size of the dot of this full stop.

Amongst fuels investigated for use where (or when) oil and petrol are scarce, scientists have tried running cars and tractors on chicken faeces.

Scientists have modified cockroaches, implanting electrodes in them to control their legs, and used them as living robots to carry cameras or explosives through tiny spaces.

Dermestid beetles are so good at stripping the flesh off dead animals that natural history museums use their larvae to clean up skeletons they are going to put on display.

a man who experimented with feeding a Venus flytrap (a type of flesh-eating plant) with bits of his own flesh found the plant could digest it easily. He used bits of his toes that had rotted and dropped off as a result of athlete's foot.

I n Chile, trains on the Arica-La Paz railway were at one time powered by burning llama faeces.

e arly matches were made of poisonous chemicals and would sometimes burst into flames on their own if they got warm and damp. They poisoned the children employed to make them, and set fire to people's pockets unexpectedly!

B acteria – tiny living things that we also call germs – divide in two every 20 minutes. So, starting with one (it doesn't need a girlfriend/boyfriend), you can have over 130 million in just 9 hours!

WORLD FACTS

THE WINNER

1st PLACE

at a single meal, obese New Yorker Walter Hudson could eat: 12 doughnuts, 10 packets of crisps, 8 Chinese take-aways and half a cake!

Charles Osbourne, from Iowa, USA, hiccupped every 1.5 seconds for 69 years and then suddenly stopped.

The most expensive coffee in the world is made with coffee beans recovered from the faeces of the *civet*, a type of wild cat from Sumatra.

Peter Dowdeswell of the UK ate a three-course meal in a record 45 seconds in 1999. He ate oxtail soup, mashed potatoes, baked beans and sausage, and then prunes.

Natasha Verushka of the USA holds female record for simultaneous sword swallowing; she held 13 in her throat at a convention in 2004.

The biggest cockroach in the world is the Madagascan hissing cockroach. It can grow to 9 centimetres (3.5 inches) – as long as an adult's finger.

Monte Pierce of the USA can flick a coin 3.3 metres (10 feet 10 inches) with his earlobes.

The black-headed sea snake found north of Australia in the Timor Sea is 100 times more deadly than the most poisonous snake on land.

Leonardo d'Andrea from Italy smashed 32 watermelons with his head in 1 minute in 2005.

Marc Quinquandon, of France, set a world record by eating 144 snails in 11 minutes. He beat his own record when he ate 72 snails in 3 minutes, but he died soon afterwards.

Kevin Cole from the USA shot a strand of spaghetti out of his nose a distance of 19 centimetres (7.5 inches) in 1998.

The biggest beetle in the world is the dung-eating Goliath beetle – it's about the size of a hamster!

The loudest recorded scream was 129 decibels, made by Jill Drake of the UK at a Halloween celebration in 2000.

In 2005, Matthew Henshaw from Australia swallowed a sword 40.5 centimetres (15.9 inches) long, and hung a sack of potatoes weighing 20 kilograms (44 pounds 5 ounces) on its handle for 5 seconds.

in 1998, 13 year-old Daniel Canal of Miami, USA, received 12 transplanted organs in only 3 weeks.

khum Chaibuddee of Thailand holds the record for kissing poisonous snakes. He kissed 19 cobras in 2006.

a Japanese woman holds the record for having most worms removed from her stomach; doctors removed a total of 56 in 1990.

A woman who worked on smelly feet in a testing laboratory had to smell 5,600 feet over 15 years.

Danny Capps holds the record for spitting a dead cricket out of his mouth, reaching a distance of 9.17 metres (30 feet).

Michael Lloyd of the USA holds the record for kicking himself in the head – 60 times in a row!

Tom Shufflebottham charmed 511 worms out of the ground at a worm-charming championship in England in 1980.

In 2008, a 9-year-old Greek girl was found to have her unborn identical twin growing inside her belly. It had a head, hair and eyes, but no brain or umbilical cord.

Norman Gary of the USA held 109 live honeybees in his mouth for 10 seconds in 1998.

Xie Qiuping of China has the world's longest hair, at 5.6 metres (18 feet, 5 inches) long.

The world's smelliest substances are two weaponised gases the US government is considering developing. They would be used to break up crowds without harming people. One of the gases is called Who Me? and the other is The US Government Standard Bathroom Malodor.

Ciro Gallo of the UK holds the record for having concrete blocks broken on his chest with a sledgehammer, while lying on a bed of nails – 37 blocks weighing a total of 235.8 kilograms (519.8 pounds).

Ken Edwards of the UK ate 36 live cockroaches in one minute on a breakfast TV show in 2001.

The longest-lasting operation took 96 hours and was carried out in Chicago, USA, in 1951 to remove a giant tumour.

Shridhar Chillal grew his fingernails for 44 years without cutting them. Their average length was 117 centimetres (46 inches), and his thumbnail was 132 centimetres (52 inches).

In 1999, American Scott Jeckel shot a marshmallow 4.96 metres (16.27 feet) out of his nose, with his friend Ray Perisin catching it in his mouth.

Robert Earl Hughes of Illinois, USA had the largest chest measurement ever recorded. He was 3.15 metres (10 feet 4 inches) around the chest when he died, aged 32. He weighed 484 kilograms (1,067 pounds).

The smallest fully grown adult ever to live was Gul Mohammed of India, who was 57 centimetres (34.5 inches) tall at the age of 33 and weighed only 17 kilograms (37.5 pounds).

after having her nose, lips and chin chewed off by her pet dog, Isabelle Dinoire received the first ever partial face transplant. In the operation, new parts from a recently deceased body were attached to her face

the record for spitting a mouthful of tobacco is 16.23 metres (53 feet 3 inches), and was set in 1997.

The longest recorded eyebrow hair was 15.1 centimetres (5.94 inches) long – and it belonged to a female!

the most poisonous fish in the world is the stone fish. Treading on its spines causes a painful death in 20 minutes.

a giant hair ball weighing 4.5 kilograms (10 pounds) was removed from the stomach of an 18-year-old American girl in 2007. It was the largest ever removed from a human body.

The worst epidemic of all time was the Black Death – a plague carried by fleas that live on rats – which killed 75 million people in Europe and Asia between 1347 and 1351.

The heaviest ever kidney stone – a solid mass of mineral that collects inside the kidneys – weighed 620 grams (21.8 ounces). It was removed from a man in Pakistan in 2008.

The longest leg hair grew on American Welsey Pemberton – it was 6.5 centimetres (6.5 inches) long.

The winner of a fly-swatting contest in 1912 killed 543,360 flies, weighing a total of 96 kilograms (212 pounds).

Kim Goodman from the USA can 'pop' her eyeballs out of their sockets so that they stick out 11 millimetres (0.4 inches).

Motorcycle stunt rider Evel Knievel of Montana, USA, held the record for broken bones – he suffered 435 fractures while working as stuntman before he died in 2007.

The world's longest nose belongs to Mehmet Ozyurek from Turkey. His conk is a whopping 8.8 centimetres (3.5 inches) long.

The youngest person to have a full set of false teeth was only 4 years old. He suffered from an inherited disease that destroyed his teeth.

American Robert Wadlow had the largest feet ever recorded. They were 47 centimetres (18.5 inches) long.

a man in Bulgaria who accidentally shot himself in 1942 still has the bullet lodged in his head.

Monte Pierce from the USA can stretch his left earlobe to a length of 12.7 centimetres (5 inches).

Garry Turner of the UK can stretch a flap of skin away from his body to a length of 15.8 centimetres (6.25 inches). He has a medical condition that affects his skin making it super-elastic.

Stephen Taylor from the UK can stick his tongue out 9.4 centimetres (3.7 inches) measured from the tip to his lips.

Shamsher Singh from India has the longest beard on a living man. In 2008, it was 1.89 metres (6 feet, 2 inches) long.

Thomas Blackthorne of the UK can lift 11 kilograms (24 pounds) of weights using just his tongue.

In 2009 Saudi man Majed al-Maliki ate 22 live scorpions in one sitting. The record holder catches them with his bare hands and eats 20 to 30 per day.

Giovanni Batista from Orsenigo, Italy, has an unusual collection of more than 2 million human teeth.

Horrible Facts

Letchemanah Ramasamy from Malaysia has pulled a double-decker bus 30 metres (around 98 feet), using only his hair.

Wim Hof of the Netherlands submerged his whole body in an ice bath for a record 1 hour 13 minutes in 2008. He used a meditation technique called *Tummo* to stop himself freezing.

Garry Turner of the UK once clipped 159 wooden clothes pegs to his face at the same time.

Frenchman Michel Lotito, aka Monsieur Mangetout (Mr Eat Everything), used to snack on all kinds of glass and metal. Before his (non-metal related) death in 2005, he'd eaten a computer, 18 bicycles, an aeroplane, 6 chandeliers, 15 supermarket trolleys, 2 beds, 7 TV sets and a pair of skis. In total, he ate more than 9 tonnes (1,984 pounds) of metal.

Jackie Bibby from the USA holds the record for sitting in a bathtub with 87 live rattlesnakes.

The largest tumour removed in one piece from a living person weighed 137.6 kilograms (303 pounds) and measured 1 metre (3 feet across). It weighed more than the woman in which it was growing.

Meng Xu of China can thread 20 needles in his mouth using just his tongue. He did it in 6 minutes and 45 seconds in 2003.

Zafar Gill of Pakistan can lift 62 kilograms (136 pounds 4 ounces) of weights with a clamp attached to his right ear.

The largest snail ever found was 39.3 centimetres (15.5 inches) long and weighed 900 grams (2 pounds).

The loudest recorded burp was produced by Paul Hunn of the UK in 2008. It measured nearly 107 decibels – as loud as a fast underground train whizzing past!

The largest rubbish tip in the world is Fresh Kills landfill, New York, USA. It is thought to contain 100 million tonnes (98 million tons) of rubbish and covers 1,200 hectares (3,000 acres).

A ribbon worm washed up on the shore of Scotland in 1864 was an incredible 55 metres (180 feet) long.

Clint Hallam from New Zealand has lost the same hand (the right one) three times – in 1984 it was cut off in an accident and doctors re-attached it; it was removed again in 1989 when it got infected; a new, transplanted hand was removed in 2001 after rejection problems.

American Gary Bashaw can mix chocolate powder and milk in his mouth and pour it out of his nose as a milkshake. In 1999, he made a record-breaking 54 millilitres (1.8 ounces) of milkshake in one go.

Over a period of 40 years, American Charles Jensen had 970 operations to remove tumours (lumps), mostly from his face.

The worst flu epidemic ever came in 1918 at the end of the First World War. It killed 21 million people – twice the amount of people who had died in the war.

a man known as **Snake Manu**, from India, swallowed 200 earthworms each at least 10 centimetres (4 inches) long in 30 seconds in 2003.

Tom Leppard from the UK has his whole body tattooed with leopard spots, with the spaces between being tattooed yellow.

in 1999, **Brad Byers of the USA** swallowed 10 swords each 68.5 centimetres (27 inches) long, and rotated them through 180 degrees in his throat.

Horrible Facts

A British woman has 6,005 body piercings including a hole in her tongue large enough to poke a finger through.

Marco Hort of Switzerland can fit 264 drinking straws in his mouth at the same time.

Kama Muk of the UK bravely had 600 new body piercings in a single day in 2002.

The fattest man in the world, Walter Hudson of New York, USA, had a waist measurement of more than 3 metres (9 feet 11 inches).

The longest recorded snake was a python 10 metres (35 feet 9.5 inches) long.

at the largest frog-leg-eating festival ever, in Florida, 2001, 13,200 people ate 3,000 kilograms (6,600 pounds) of frogs' legs fried in batter.

The heaviest living snake is a Burmese python that weighs nearly 183 kilograms (403 pounds) and is 71 centimetres (28 inches) round. It lives in a safari park in the USA.

The fastest eater is the starnosed mole. It can identify something as edible, catch and eat it in 120 milliseconds.

The largest jellyfish was 2.28 metres (7 feet 6 inches) across its body and had a tentacle span of 36.5 metres (120 feet).

Dean Gould of England can pick 50 winkles (a shellfish like a small snail) from shells with a pin in 1 minute 22 seconds.

Andy Szerbini of the UK holds the record for eating baked beans with a cocktail stick – he ate 226 in 5 minutes.

During heart surgery in 1970, a patient with haemophilia (an inherited condition which stops the blood clotting) needed 1,080 litres of blood – nearly 15 baths full – as he kept bleeding

By March 2005, American Donald Gorske had eaten 20,500 Big Macs. He has eaten at least one a day for 33 years.

Dustin Phillips of the USA can drink a whole bottle of tomato ketchup through a straw in only 33 seconds.

The longest beard ever was grown by Hans Langseth of Norway, whose whiskers stretched an incredible 5.33 metres (17.6 feet) when measured on his death in Kensett, Iowa, in 1927. The beard was presented to the Smithsonian Institution, Washington DC, in 1967.

The most expensive soup is made with shark's fin, sea cucumbers and other yucky (and illegal) stuff. *Buddha-jumps-over-the-wall* soup costs £108 and has to be ordered five days in advance.

The most poisonous animal in the world is probably the two-toned arrow-poison frog – only 28 grams (1 ounce) of its poison could kill nearly 3 million people.

american Jon Brower Minnoch was the heaviest man ever recorded in history. At his heaviest, he weighed 635 kilograms (1,400 pounds). He was so fat that it took 12 firemen to lift him out of his house when he fell ill, and 13 nurses to turn him over in bed. In fact, he had two beds strapped together as one wasn't big enough to hold him. He once put on 89 kilograms (196 pounds) in a single week.